Women to Women

Sisters of Sarah

Nadia Watson-Anthony

Greatness University Publishers
info@greatness-university.com
www.greatness-university.com

ISBN: 978-1-913164-67-6
ISBN-13:978-1-913164-67-6

CONTENTS

ACKNOWLEDGMENTS

To every woman who suffered any kind of abuse, for the nights in the dark, the days on earth in hell, and the evenings of being in prison in your own minds-keep living the life, sisters this is just the beginning!

Special Note from Author

Women to women keep the Christ-like attitude and remember that we are not only daughters of Sarah we are sisters. It is because of this lift each other up. Are you ready to look at life differently? Are you ready to read stories that will change your life? Are you ready to get the tools you need to start that business, build that relationship, write that next book? I am glad you said "Yes" to all of my questions. Let's enter into another amazing book that will give you assurance that we are sisters of Sarah and we too will reap the harvest and benefit of everything God has in store for us.

Introduction

Nadia Watson-Anthony
Master of Greatness

Introduction

A place that you can go to tape in the life of women and business all at one time. As you journey through this book of reflection you will find details and information concerning how to better yourself, your business and deal with circumstances that will come your way. *"It's all up to you how you use it."* For decades women in general have been abused, unappreciated, Overlooked, overloaded and underrepresented. Today I come to represent and look into the lives of women. Reading these testimonies and informative messages will provoke you to become more powerful and comfortable in who God has made you, that is partly because each woman in this collection speaks from a place of hard one enlightenment.

Many women and this book have gone through unimaginable circumstances and have experienced things that you can relate too, but the thing that I love about each woman is that they all have faith, resilience and a mighty heart that wants to encourage the people of God. Sherica Thompson teaches us how to gain roof top access. Siemone Anthony gives us insight on *"The Truth that REALLY hurts- The Sarah in my life."* Raine Diane Fossett talks about *"Give me a piece of that peace!"* In turn Ida Newton, breakdown the life of Sarah motivating us by saying, *"Don't trip."* Donna Yaeger builds a relationship with her brother. Powerful evangelistic Nicole Ajibola shares a life changing moment that leads her to Jesus. Talesiya Calton Shares ``how *time was stolen from her precious family and friends"* in the meantime Latonya Neal shares ``What *is absent, is Really present.*" Touching the heart of abused woman LuWanna Riles gives us insight on how she survived an abusive relationship. Sisters of Sarah, it is not easy to pick up a pen and write your life sometimes going back into your past hurts.

Don't be afraid to work hard and realize that sometimes the smallest and the darkest dirtiest jobs are often the most important. -Alice Waters

Now, writing this letter to you he's going to force me to think pretty deeply about my life, and you know thinking deeply was never one of your favorite activities."- Dale Earnhardt Jr.

The biggest adventure you can ever take is to live the life of your dreams. - Oprah Winfrey

As you continue to read, take in the nourishment, inspiration and motivation. Sisters, grab your popcorn, tissues and a cold beverage and be prepared to tap into the lives of strong woman 'Sisters of Sarah.'

Wife verses Babymama

Sarah was one of those women whom King Lemuel spoke about. Sarah did her husband good and not evil all the days of her life. (Prov. 31:12).

The bible gives us what we need in order to face this thing we call life although, we do not like to talk about certain subjects

"Can you believe this situation?" Sarah is a woman that has been called to the heights of all women. A woman that had to go through a trial in order to get what God had for her. God promises that Sarah would be the mother of his nation but the thing is Sarah has a problem we would say. Sarah was barren and old in fact, the bible says that Sarah and Abraham find the whole thing to be very funny. (17:17; 18:11) have you ever had a good laugh at your situation? If not start laughing because God is in control.

Sarah thought her husband needed a child. Well, at least thought it was a great plan Genesis 16. We all know the story! Sarah took the matter into her own hands, she hands her own hand made Hagar over to Abraham, saying, "it may be that I shall obtain children by her " (16:2). If you continue reading the bible says everything went as she had planned. Hagar has a son by the name of Ishmael but there is one problem, Sarah did not anticipate all the family-drama and serious family problems that would result from her behaviour of Hagar, in fact Sarah had no idea the storm she was about to walk in. Reflect for a moment, "What storm have you put yourself in?" Think about a time that you went before god. "How did things turn out for you?" Hagar, who moves up the ladder from baby mama to wife status (main chick) with a son. "did you say she had a son?" OH no!! Sarah. As you can see, Sarah has taken matters into her own hands. "Can you recall a time when you took matters into your own hands?" I can, it was like yesterday I remember dating a guy and because i thought I was in love I gave him my most precious valued piece of gold " my car." That's right ladies, I let this man use my car and he wrecked it. Now, this may seem small to you but I was hurt. I thought I knew love and because I wanted him so bad I started doing crazy things like allowing him to enter into my place of peace, this rolled over into my adulthood causing pain, sleepless night, depression, and a whole bunch of doubt. There are a lot of things I had to experience because I decided to take matters into my own hands which brings me to my next question. "Who have you given your all to that brought you a trial that rolled over into your adulthood?"

With all the problems Sarah had created she hurry up and tries to remove Hagar and ruins her new status as companion (main chick)

With all that happens in Sarah's life, the lord still finds a way to save her from her situation and he started with changing Sarah's name. In order for you to reap the full benefit of God's blessing in your life, you are going to have to change your mind. Yes, you have fallen short but we all have. "You know what time it is? It's time to change your name, in the bible when God changed a person's name and gave them a new name, it was usually to establish their new identity in him. In the secular world parents are coming up with creative names like Liv and Liam, but back in the day, names weren't as trendy. However, lots of female celebrities chose to re-name themselves to better brand themselves and create a new identity that seemed to resonate with who they are and how they wanted their name to come to light in Hollywood. "What is your new name?" "How do you want god and the world to view you and your new name?"

God changed Abram's name to "Abraham," "father of a multitude" (Genesis 17:5) tells us. God also changed his wife's name from "Sarai," to "Sarah," Genesis 17:15– • Sarah: meaning "When God Is Silent." Genesis 16:1-9.

Women to Women do you know that the most difficult times in our life is when God is silent. In those silent times we have a choice. That choice is to wait on God or go with our own plans.

As hardworking women striving to be better everyday must learn to be patient and wait on our God. Sarah was a woman in the bible who learned that it is hard to wait on God especially when he is silent. This story has so much power, without this story us as women would have thought Sarah was perfect right? A great woman can only be that kind of wife, mother, and friend when she believes that nothing is too difficult or too big for God.

Faced with a serious decision, Sarah again does what any other wise women would consider doing and that is. Sarah tries to remove the problem, the problem she created for herself; Hagar. Sarah ruined Hagar's new status as the main chick. Come on ladies! Once Sarah persuades Abraham to put Hagar under her Authority as she was before, Sarah mistreats the poor woman woman, who's suffering so badly that she runs away with her child the bible tells us (16:6-7). And you know what? That was probably not Sarah's intention at all but, but because she went before God Sarah had to do something. Are you the baby mama or the wife? I can tell you that I'm both and I'm all about making and keeping the peace. Sarah probably was starting to feel threatened, living with A woman that has her husband's son. Have you been faced with this kind of problem? Sisters or shall I say sistas, the bible gives us what we need in order to face this thing we call life although, we don't like to talk about certain subjects we have to be honest with circumstances such as this. Can you believe this situation! Sarah a woman that has been called to the heights of all women. A woman that had to go through in order to get what God had for her. My sisters, you are all beautiful and privileged woman as well, no matter what you have been through you must consider the fact that the Lord is with you. If God is silent in your life please wait and be patient; and in the meantime, continue to pray holding fast to the promises of God knowing that he his answers or sometimes silent and sometimes they are loud. It's up to you to determine when God speaks to your heart so pay close attention not being deceived by Satan and our own fleshly desires.

1 Corinthians 10:13 New International Version (NIV) No temptation[a] has overtaken you except what is common to mankind. And God is faithful; he will not let you be tempted[b] beyond what you can bear. But when you are tempted,[c] he will also provide a way out so that you can endure it.

Prayer: *Make it Personal*

oh Father, I thank You because my past shows me that with You, I will always be blessed.know matter how many times I am tempted lord I know you will allow a way out. lord I thank you for your grace and mercy, lord you are the same God You were in the past; therefore, I know that I can trust in You for my future. I thank You for the blessings I will experience, the tribulations I will overcome, the things that You will reveal and the wisdom You will give me over time. So right now, I thank You in advance, Amen.

Sisters of Sarah

Be thankful for what you have; you'll end up having more. If you concentrate on what you don't have, you will never, ever have enough. -Oprah Winfrey

Prayer: *Corporate Prayer*

Our Father who is in heaven, thank You for equipping us to stand together as sisters. Thank you for also equipping us to stand against the plans of the enemy. Thank You for the armor that will help us to be victorious in your Name Jesus . Oh Lord, thank You for giving us the strength to overcome the battles that we have not yet faced. We thank You for the deliverance we will experience because of your Word which is everlasting, thank you for providing the nursment in order to keep Christ alive in our lives. Thank you father and lord we stretch out our hands and look to the hills for which cometh our help, we know that our help comes from you.

Amen.

Sisters of Sarah

Building a Relationship

Donna Lloy Yaeger

Donna Lloy Yaeger was born in Washington State in the middle 1950's. She grew up among a family with difficulties typical of those trying to realize the American dream, but falling short time and again. As with most families, a technique of hiding what is real behind a narrative generated to fit expectations resulted. Turbulent teen years filled with disappointments was followed by a marriage to a repeatedly unfaithful husband led Donna to place far from love and God's purpose. But that's not the end of the story.

A chance for a new life came upon meeting her future husband and the opportunity to come to know Jesus in a real and profound way. Through a career that ended prematurely and the sufferings of learning to walk by faith, her story is one of both trial and victory. Come into her life and share her experiences to see how Christ offers love and opens doors. It is a story of victory found only in a loving savior.

When the snow melts in Montana the April showers are generally slushy snow and chilly evenings. The rivers are still thawing, the crocuses are still poking through mounds of white stuff and the grass is not green. The trees do not dare sprout leaves yet, but the native Montanan's know spring is near.

My husband and I look forward to digging in the garage to search for the lawn furniture. We sweep off the patio and set up the outdoor heater for the chilly evenings we bundle up for our first evening dinner on the patio.

We are brave as we shop for those hearty nursery flowers that will survive the next few months on the patio. We listen carefully for the weatherman's forecast warning for the temperatures dipping too low, snow threats, we will take them into warmer shelter, cover them with blankets, or tell ourselves they need to toughen up. It is not until the end of May before it is safe for seedlings to be planted in the ground for fear of the killing frost to spoil a good plant. We are very proud of our eight hanging flower baskets on the roof lines of the garage and house, it all makes for a lot of babysitting during surprise storms. But when all the flowers are full of blossoms during the summer and the hummingbirds, bees and butterflies are active we are very proud of all our hard work.

Most Montanan's have a saying about our summers, we only have, "Construction and Company"! Luckily my husband's family lives here in Montana and my family rarely comes to visit, this made me very shocked when I got a call from my big brother asking if he could come stay for the month of May to do some fishing. My husband's schedule would keep him out of town for a couple weeks, so it would be up to me to entertain my brother and arrange for our friends, who had a drift boat, to take my brother fly fishing if they had time. So, of course I said, "Yes!" told my brother it would be just the two dogs and me, at least until my husband got home from business in Kalispell. My brother said, "Perfect, I leave tomorrow."

Three years ago, I became very ill and my brother and his family hosted us as we traveled into the Big City to one of the major medical facilities for tests. We stayed for a week and traveled back and forth with different specialists for appointments, it was quite a grueling affair. My brother's wife is a Registered Nurse, working in the surgical ward at the local Hospital, so she was compassionate and full of questions upon our return from our long day pursuit for answers. There was no hesitation in providing the same hospitality or better for my brother now. I was looking forward to seeing him. The doorbell rang, the two dogs rushed the door. It was their duty as greeters, I opened the door and I couldn't help myself as tears welled up in my throat when I saw my brother's face and big grin. A tangle of dog legs and both of us wrapped our arms around each other as we cried in our uncomfortable long embrace, we wiped our tears, a chuckled with embarrassment to the ease of our emotion seeing one another.

"Where are your bags?"

"Here on the porch." He had piled five large bags, fishing gear and boots all on the front porch. I tried not to be surprised, he was planning more than a fishing trip. My heart told me something deeper was troubling my brother.

"Well, let's get you settled into the guest room and rested from the long drive. It is so good to see you!"

The silly setter and Westie made him feel right at home. The Westie sits on her hind feet and waves with both front feet until you speak to her personally. As my brother put his things away I could hear him talking to them and laughing downstairs entertained by the clowns. I could hear the specific toys they had brought for him by the unique squeakers.

As he was topping the stairs I shouted a warning, "Be careful the dogs will race you to the top of the stairs and trip you." They shot out the doggy door as the stairs reached the top before turning into the kitchen.

My brother had a traveling cooler from his road food, I opened up the refrigerator door and told him the dinner plans for the evening pointing to an empty shelf he could use for his things.

"Elk steaks are over there marinating, a bottle of Merlot is breathing, a nice green salad, I make my own salad dressing, I hope you will like it, and fresh hard rolls. There is more wine in the basement, too, we could pull another cork in anticipation, or I could go get beer-if you would prefer?" I was talking fast and feeling nervous. I don't know why. We carried everything outside to the patio, and started the charcoals for a good hot grill.

The evening was perfect, I did not have to fuss with the outdoor heater the temperature had warmed up to 70 degree with beautiful blue sky, the bees and birds were singing to us and enjoying our flowers. The neighbor has lilacs bushes that border our fence line and May is when they start blooming, the fragrance was filling the evening air, it was intoxicating as we emptied or first bottle of wine and opened our second. The dogs each received a small Elk steak of their own chopped into their dog food. They brought their squeaky toys for my brother to throw and like good retrievers they returned them faithfully. We put the grill away, carried the dishes inside, filled the dishwasher and took the bottle of wine and glasses to the living room. We settled onto the large leather couch across from each other and sat the wine bottle on the coffee table. The Westie jumped up on my lap gently, she knew how to snuggle. But the Silly Setter was younger and all legs, tail and wavy skirts! The Westie had to growl at her to make her calm down, when reprimanded there was an immediate flop!! We were all content in our places and my brother laughed at the display of leadership.

I smiled, "She's the boss!" just then the Westie filled her cheeks making a sound like an old lady huffing,

Directed at my brother, "uff, uff!!" then she put her head down on my lap adjusted her shoulders and closed her eyes.

My brother snickered, "I guess she just had the last word."

"You've been told, don't be laughing, this is serious discipline." Just then the setter let out a big sigh!

Our conversation took on questions about our youth, our relatives, how we were educated, mostly our lack of social skills and how we had good friends that taught us, rather their families taught us how not to be barbarians. He asked me questions that I had been asking myself for a long time, such as, did I see what he saw? Was I aware of our home upbringing and the way we were raised, he was asking for my memories because he said our sister changes history all the time it never stays the same, it changes to suit her needs. I finally had to speak up and share the truth of my story with him I was not around in the teen years. I was not able to have a full childhood. I was sent away and was never re-incorporated back into the family, those twenty years were lost to me. The truth of it at 15 I had to grow up fast, search for a way out, Dad deserted the ship and Mom sent me away and never looked back, just said to me as she dumped me in the Big City, "Everyone thinks you are going to fail, they think I am crazy, you are too young, don't make me look foolish." I succeeded. I graduated with high scores at the age of 17 among twenty-year olds. The Dean of the NorthWestern College kept his eye on me and spoke to me often, asked the instructors how I was doing. I had opportunities to work at Swedish Hospital Laboratory. I should have stayed there, the Dean of NW College would have signed for me and Swedish had a High School program, it would have worked out for me to stay. Mom was going to show me off by bringing me back home, make sure everyone knew I had successfully completed the program. I was still only seventeen so she changed my birth certificate to 18, I had six months to go. Just like the abortion, this was all about her clearing her good name, not about protecting her daughter. She was trying to hide the shame of her family not protect her daughter from a perpetrator that she allowed in her home. Dad told me no one would have me; I should just marry the man that abused me, no one else would take me, I was spoiled goods. Then when I got the job at the Laboratory under false pretenses and the Lab supervisor showed interest in me Dad was shocked. So he married me off to him. I did not love him, he was a manipulator, he was always with other women, the day before my wedding he was with another woman, I knew he could never love me, I was his third wife. My Dad said I would never go without shoes. I went without love and I had the same shoes I had when I married him nine years later when the divorce papers were final. I left him three times; the third time was to join the Army. I put myself through college and I could do it again. I enjoyed laboratory work but, in the Army, I had to change career moves to Diagnostic Imaging, by making that happen I met my husband, moved to Montana and dropped off the planet and got away from my family. When I asked for help my father was resistant. My mother tried to help but my father was angry. As I departed with all my possessions in a 1972 Valiant Plymouth and two cats in the dead of winter, I tried to say goodbye to my father and he would not look at me. He was at my sister's house hammering a picture on the wall. I took the hammer out of his hand and said I wanted to say goodbye but he would not look at me. His face was cold and hateful. I walked out the door with the picture of his hate on my mind.

My brother began to enlighten me on what my sister had done from the time I had left. All the family had gone through because of her. She had married five times. They knew of two annulments when she was in Alaska that was sketchy, if she had not had her young daughter my parents would have left her up there. She came home in pretty bad shape. Dad had bought homes for her, moved men out of their homes, repaired homes they had bought for her, in the meantime became property owners because of her and had basically raised her other two children. While I remember my mother telling me she would not raise my bastard child if I chose to give birth. The oldest grandchild was beaten up by my sister and our mom was also beaten up and went to the police station to have pictures taken of their bruises and cut lips. Grandma had custody of the oldest grandchild. I had no idea! It was so sad to hear all these things and yet my father was ashamed of me? My sister was on drugs, sleeping with men, they could not find her and would come get the children because they were often alone, good thing they knew how to dial the phone. I told my brother I am not sure I wish to know anymore because my father's hatred for me makes no sense.

"That is why I am here, everything in our family is such a lie. I am full up here trying to make sense of my own lies. My marriage is a lie. My kids are screwed up. I am a mess. I need to know what happened, Sis, I never knew!"

I took a deep breath, "How much do you know?"

"What I heard in the locker room."

"No one ever asked. They believed the worst of me and they poured their shame, blame and hate on me."

My brother's eyes were filled with tears, "I know it has haunted me, like a black cloud. I am so sorry I brought him home, Mom should not have let him stay."

"No, our parents had a responsibility to their teenage daughters, he was nineteen years old, a drunk, a rebel, a manipulator, a liar, taking advantage of our whole family, you especially. No, he should have gone home that night and apologized to his mother and father for beating them up."

"Are you sure you want to hear, everyone has told their version of 'My Story'?" I was petting the Westie's back looking down focusing on something trying not to cry. 'Where do I start?"

Memories of my brother how he had run away for those months during the fateful call from the Doctor's office when mom got the call that the pregnancy test was positive. I was not even aware the Doctor had taken a blood test because he thought I was pregnant.

I was home recovering from an Urethrotomy procedure because as a child I had chronic UTI's and this was a way the Doctor chose to help me correct my Bladder infections. My brother's friend was skipping school and showed up at the house while I was convalescing. I was in my pajamas alone. He asked me what I was doing home from school and I was too embarrassed to answer him. He hardly spoke to me. I was tall, skinny, shy and never had been kissed, had never been with a boyfriend and was very awkward socially. He sat next to me on the couch and started petting my leg and I moved away from him. He put his arm around me and I moved his arm off of my shoulder. He jumped back and said, "Damn you are a virgin!!" I jumped up beat red and grabbed my robe around my neck and answered him, "So what if I am!" He grabbed me, kissed me saying, "I never kissed a virgin, I never knew they even existed!" I ran to my bedroom and shut the door. We were alone in the house. My heart was beating fast and I was frightened. He knocked on the door, I did not answer, he pushed on the door, the door sticks and I huddled up close to the wall hoping he would go away. I said nothing.

Then he talked to mom about taking me to a movie. I wanted to see this movie and I never did anything, I always just stayed in my room, a homebody, an introvert. HE WAS A LIAR. He took me down to the river bank, he had his older brother's station wagon. He had planned the whole thing was premeditated. We wrestled and I tried to get away, he kept telling me I would like it, and I told him no many times, he even insulted my body telling me I had no boobies yet, but that was to be expected since I was still a virgin. I know I could have run; I was scared, it was dark. Then when he had his way with me, he had the nerve to tell me I was not a virgin, because he had not felt anything. I cried. He dropped me off at my house and drove away. Mom was sitting in her chair, all she said was the movie out early. I went to the bathroom avoiding the mirror, I cleaned myself up and went to my bed and cried myself to sleep. I threw away my outfit I wore. I stayed in my room and did not interact with the family. I was nauseated and sick to my stomach every time I heard his voice. When he heard I was pregnant he said he wanted to marry me and that made me sick. Then dad said no one else would have me and that scared me because I wanted children. I would lay there in my bed and just cry myself to sleep.

The Abortionist memories were painful, too, they used only valium injections back then, I was conscious for the entire procedure. When the speculum was inserted the Doctor was concerned calling the nurse over to look at this and scooted out of the way for her to look, her hymen is still there. I was fully aware because I thought something was wrong with me. I laid there really still with my eyes closed repeating the word to myself. He asked her for a scalpel and she brought him a big clamp. He told me this is going to make you feel like you have really bad cramps. Before he did anything, the nurse monitoring my blood pressure wanted to see because the Nurse had been whispering in her ear, so the Doctor showed her. I was crying and asked what was wrong? The Doctor scolded the ladies, clamped down with the device that was inserted, all I heard was the roar of the machine. It all hurt like lightning, the top of my head, my pelvis and I felt numb all over. Afterwards, the Abortion Doctor wanted to talk to me. I was helped to the dressing room. I was very light headed. The nurse that was checking my blood pressure came back to escort me to his office, he was seated behind his desk. He asked me who brought me to the clinic. I told him my mom, she was waiting in the car in the parking lot. He asked me about the man who had gotten me pregnant and I blushed, he said let's just skip the details of all that I just want to explain something to you. Whoever penetrated you was not very big. He was too small for your vagina. He showed me a model of a vagina, hymen, cervix, uterus and ovaries. He explained to me a man's penis needs to penetrate the hymen in order to allow semen to fertilize the egg. In your circumstance young lady it is almost an immaculate conception, then he smiled at me. I blushed and said I do not understand. He walked over to the chair next to me and took my hand, looked into my eyes and very seriously said you have had no formal religious training or sexual education. A tear ran down my cheek. He wiped it away with his thumb as he pulled me up from my chair. He said one final thing to me before he saw me out of his office. Trust me the sexual experience you had was not normal. He was too small for you, choose a taller man next time it will be more enjoyable. Good luck with your future, you seem like a sweet kid. When I returned to the parking lot mom had seen me go into the Doctor's office and asked me what the Doctor had told me, I gave her many evasive responses but I could never lie to my mom, she just knew, so I told her what he said. She slammed the car door stomped into the Clinic, I called after her standing in the parking lot begging her not to go, I could hear her screaming. When she returned, she peeled out of the parking lot like a race car driver.

I avoided everyone at school, just went to my classes. Then boys I did not know started showing up at my locker rubbing up against me saying, 'I am next', and crude things and vulgar things to me. I would hide in the girl's bathroom until my next class and run across campus to avoid contact with anyone. Then I started having burning urination and the Doctor had told me if I had problems come and leave him a specimen in his office. So, I walked to the Doctor's office, (being a small community everything is within walking distance) talked to the nurse and told her. She did her dip Styx thing and told me to wait for the Doctor to take a look at you. Well, he did the BIG BAD SPECULUM!! Then they drew blood and I being young and vulnerable let them. This is before the privacy acts and mom gets the call a couple of weeks later. I walk home from school and mom is screaming at me hysterically, hitting me with a broom, yelling at me who is he, how dare you, I thought you were a good girl and sat down exhausted crying and I still have no idea what is wrong. I am in my room scared to death. My mom had a hysterectomy really early in her life and all three of us children recognized her as needing her hormone shot and she would go CRAZY like this … but never this bad!! The other siblings would put it on me to hint to her she needs to go get her shot, well I would draw pictures, leave a poem or iron all the clothes in the ironing basket with a sweet note saying, "Now would be a good time to go get your shot!" But no way in HELL am I leaving my room to face this Tasmanian devil to find out what that was about.

I looked up at my brother, "I am sorry about your marriage. Are you running away now like you did then? I don't want you to get in trouble for being here."

"Low blow, I deserved that. No, my family knows I am taking time off and they know I am here. "

"Good!"

"I have been running from a lot of crap, but when I heard you could not have children because of the abortion that broke my heart. Both of you would make such great parents." We both broke down crying. "When you stayed at our house you both have such a love for each other, look at these dogs, you have so much to give. My marriage sucks, my kids are spoiled rotten."

"We have Christ, it has not been easy, our careers, being on call... You just built that beautiful home.

Your wife just graduated nursing school, her dream job. The kids are in High School, college is around the corner. All your prestigious friends you had over for the seafood barbeque on your deck they all seem to value you. Your plans for Real Estate and Financial bond classes when you retire from your job."

"Pipe dreams, Sis." My brother finished his glass of wine and poured himself another, "We are so far in debt we live so high and beyond our means now, my wife and kids have no idea how to stop spending, I do not know how to tell them we are broke."

The dogs barked, jumped off the couch, we heard the doggy door slap and we could hear them outside. It startled us and it gave us a moment to re-adjust and change the subject.

"So, I came partly to apologize for all those years-that fateful day that changed your life when I brought my friend home. I am so sorry that Bastard hurt you!" My brother started tearing up.

I leaned over towards him and put my hand on his shoulder. I knew I would need a box of Kleenex so I got one off the other end table. Just then the dogs returned. As I sat back down next to my brother the Setter stood on me and the Westie sat where I was sitting and the Setter's tail hit my brother in the face and we started to laugh as we were blowing our nose's as we dodged legs and tails, being walked on. Luckily my brother welcomed the interruption as he grabbed the silly setter and hugged her getting a big tongue on his cheek.

Once we settled back on the couch my brother's face was full of compassion as I unloaded, not quite knowing how to begin my story of the shame, pain and blame from my family all those years. But my brother had come for closure and healing. My successes were coming to Montana finding a wonderful man that loved me, the blessing of finding the Lord and all the abundance of what that brought into my life now. Hoping the wine, our maturity, our security of having survived all those years would make my story less painful I sighed said a prayer and began.

"It was being taken advantage of that hurts the worst. A conquest from your friend, worst of all he took advantage of our whole family. Our parents took him into our home and he disrespected them by abusing me. Then our parents did not protect me by allowing a man nineteen years old to live under their roof with two teenage daughters. There were so many mistakes. It was not your fault and there is no way you should be carrying any part of their guilt."

The abortion tore my uterus free from the wall of my abdomen. I had a procedure called a Salpingogram. It showed a free-floating ovaries and uterus literally dangling in my pelvis. I was sterile. My eggs would basically go out into my abdomen not finding my uterus to be fertilized. When I had my hysterectomy the doctor found endometriosis, fibroids, adhesions, and my ovaries were upside down spilling out into my abdominal cavity. No wonder my menstrual cycles were so painful. All the fertility procedures never worked. I was crying and trying to keep my voice clear as I explained making sense of a painful outcome with years of hope.

My brother leaned over taking my hand as I could no longer hold it in, I was sobbing now, saying it openly, "My husband's mother was so disappointed I could not give her son a baby I could see it in her face, he would have made such a good daddy!" The Westie was licking my tears off my chin.

"Why I had to suffer this shame alone is something I have searched in my heart to forgive my parents and my family, my Lord and God has helped me find this peace. It has been so hard. They wanted to hide the shame from the community. They wanted to get rid of any sign of what had happened to me. They were willing to raise my sister's children but not mine. I had no choice in the matter... my fate was sealed; my mother's mind was made up and abortion was the only option. I only fought for my survival to leave the area to send me away, do not leave me in school to be ridiculed or tormented further. Your friend was bragging about what he had done to me. My sister was writing letters telling everyone. I told Mom after school one day when she picked us up from school, she slapped me across the face telling me do not bring your sister down to your level. If I stayed in that nasty little town I would drop out or commit suicide out of shame. No one would listen to me or talk to me. Not even you, you ran away believing the worst of me, I thought we were close. I do remember when I started taking night classes to apply for graduating classes early so I could go to the NW college program, I was belittling myself and you chased after me, it meant so much to me then. I thank you for the pep talk, it got me through the hard times."

"I remember Dad took me and your friend to the basement for a private conversation, he wanted to know if your friend was willing to marry me, he said yes, but I was not willing. Dad said I would not get a better offer, no one would have me, I was spoiled goods and I better take his offer."

"When I told mom, what happened she went crazy and threatened him and your friend joined the Army!" They were crazy times and your friend was gone soon after that.

It was two in the morning and we were both exhausted, stifling our yawns.

"Let's chase these pups outside and go to bed!"

We stood outside under the Big Montana Sky full of stars looking up, quiet not saying a word, sniffling to ourselves. The dogs put themselves to bed as we heard the slap of the doggy door behind them. We followed them and stood at the top of the basement stairs.

We hugged each other and said good night. "I love you big brother, I am glad you came." "Me too, thank you, Sis." As he headed downstairs. The dogs were in their designated spots on the bed yawning. I brushed my teeth crawled into bed and they snuggled up tight. As I laid awake thinking of the night's discussion, I remembered the story mom had told me over and over again about when she brought me home from the Hospital.

Grama was staying helping her while she was home with me. Mom had pneumonia when she was pregnant with me. My brother wanted to hold me so badly. Grama grabbed the camera and said why not let him hold his sister. Mom was not sure about letting him. Grama finally talked mom into it and made my brother sit quietly on the couch. Grama was ready with the camera. Both ladies were very apprehensive about a two-year-old and newborn baby, I was so frail and sickly. Mom laid me in my brother's arms and as soon as I saw his face my eyes opened wide and my hand reached up and touched his face. My mom gasped and my Grandma said, "Did you see that?" My mom had to grab the camera away from Grandma to get the picture. My brother was grinning as he said, "I've been waiting for you!" It was like we knew each other. It was like we had been reunited from something or some place, no one could understand but us. It was magical. My mom and Grandma would retell the story over and over to us when we were older. My brother was so gentle with me. They had never seen a newborn smile or open their eyes. I was so aware I recognized him and touched his face with my tiny hand. It was an amazing moment they relieved and retold.

Tonight, was like that, too. We had been reunited. The past had hurt us. But the air had been cleared. Forgiveness and pain had been wiped away. Whatever my brother had come searching for I hope he had found some answers. I loved him, I loved him for being brave, for being vulnerable, for coming to ask, for wanting to know the truth. My brother stayed longer than a month. He and my husband fished together with our friends. We had Bible studies, went to Church together, we shared many more meals on the patio and my brother accepted Christ as his Savior. He truly learned the truth has been forgiven and we have been united as heavenly brother and sister. Those infants knew something we did not know, but our Lord knows. We are bonded for all eternity now!

Don't Trip

Ida Newton Crenshaw

Ida has 3 beautiful daughters, 1 son and a grandmother of 6 and great grandmother of 6, she loves to write and manages her own business. Ida is currently living her best life in the state of Texas. This beautiful woman of god has a passion that has carried her through this life and she is amazingly grateful to inspire you to become a better person. Ida loves you and most of all our lord Jesus Christ.

Laugh at my pain

When Sarah conceived a child, she was 90 years old. God promised Abraham that she would be "a mother of nations" (Genesis 17:16) and that she would conceive and bear a son, But Sarah did not believe.

What are you believing in God for?

Sarah was so Beautiful Abraham feared she would be killed so he pretended to be Sarah Brother (Genesis 12:11-13)

Do you know that you are beautiful as well?

How often do you tell yourself that you are a masterpiece of god? Sarah and Abraham had a sense of humor God approached them about giving birth to a Son, they both laughed hysterically. How often do you laugh at life?

How often do you enjoy a good laugh with friends? Woman to Woman "Sisters of Sarah"

Abraham fell on his face and laughed while "Sarah laughed to herself" Sarah and Abraham we're getting ready to birth a promise child. Take a moment and think about your age. Do you think you're too old to birth out something that god has promised? Truth is, if god has said it must be true! Sarah was 90 years old when Isaac was born. As you can see Abraham and Sarah were quite old when Sarah became pregnant naming their son Isaac, which means "Laughter "There was no natural way possible that they could conceive a child. Abraham exclaimed, shall a child be born to a man who is a hundred years old? Shall Sarah, who is ninety years old, bear a child? (Gen 17:17). Sarah a mother of all nations who had to come to reality becoming a mother at 90. Because she was looking at the outer beauty of her body instead of the inner side which caused her to lack faith.

What is stopping you?

How can you trust god more?

Trust is a valued character trait often lacking in today's world. We have to learn to trust God in every circumstance and in every area of our lives.

Joshua 1:9 (ESV) Have I not commanded you? Be strong and courageous. Do not be frightened, and do not be dismayed, for the LORD your God is with you wherever you go."

With that being said, her husband was over 100 years old and probably not hot himself. As I stated earlier, she felt like God had ·to be kidding or had made a huge mistake.

Psalm 28:7

"The LORD is my strength and my shield; in him my heart trusts, and I am helped; my heart exults, and with my song I give thanks to him."

The Good News from Ida: When we put our faith in God, He will find great ways to return that trust. He will guide us and protect us always.

I can relate to Sarah, I'm sixty-years-old, I've been through A few things like being molested, and my life being threatened at gunpoint, But God! God said to trust him with my life and he would bless me abundantly. Here's the thing... Sarah was a walking miracle just like you and I. Her path was already mapped out by God just like you and I.

God tells them Both they are going to be parents and they both laugh hysterically. With everything I've been through I sit back and laugh at my pain.

I'm not laughing because it's funny, I'm laughing because I didn't think I would see this day, and in a sense, it is kind of funny because I doubted god and he showed up yet again. I'm now 60 years old setting goals, writing books and becoming co-author of this book. My god! Sometimes you have to sit back and just take a deep breath laughing at your pains because "what God has for you, is for you. "No matter how old you are god will grant you gains if you just hold on.

So, are you thinking about taking a big laugh at your pain? Because I'm laughing at your pain with all due respect, I know God will see you through this. No matter what it looks like, no matter the mistakes you have made the lord will see you through. Sisters we are not only sisters, we are daughters as well.

I hope You decide to take that good (laugh)because god has the last say so.

Romans 8:28

"And we know that for those who love God all things work together for good."

The Good News from Ida: We may not understand God's big plan, but we should trust that He has one for us. Everything in our lives happens that way for His reason.

God told me, to tell myself that I would get through my storms, I would write a book, I would finish school, I would be successful at 60 and guess what I did "I laughed at the thought."

I remember the day and the laugh, with all my doubts I laughed and walked across the stage at 55 with my diploma in my hand. I'm in the midst of my degree now.

Ask yourself this question, where am I in my Life? What are my goals? Where is my faith?

Don't Trip

First of all, "Don't Trip" you may be saying to yourself. I can't do it, I don't have the time, or I work too much, my children still need me, STOP IT!

If you had the time to ask yourself all of these questions you have time to change your life.

Psalm 62:8

"Trust in him at all times, oh people; pour out your heart before him; God is a refuge for us."

The Good News from Ida: It's easy to trust God when things are going well, but we must believe in Him in all times — good or bad. He will be there for us through it all.

Yes, we do work a lot and we will always work unless we start taking time for us (ME). Why? Because it's not that we think we are better than anyone else, We just want to do better for ourselves and There is Nothing wrong with that. As for our children they will always need us no matter how old they are...

Matthew 6:25 ESV

"Therefore, I tell you, do not be anxious about your life, what you will eat or what you will drink, nor about your body, what you will put on. Is not life more than food, and the body more than clothing?

Freedom

Remember we live in a country where we can do anything, you can have a business, you can become a doctor, nurse. You can do almost anything, but the truth be told we can't do anything without God and faith.

Psalm 46:10 ESV

"Be still, and know that I am God. I will be exalted among the nations; I will be exalted in the earth!"

If you set your goals and standard high, you can become the president of the United States. (Laugh) now, look around you, anyone can become president. I'LL WAIT.... (laugh)

sisters of Sarah we must stop sabotaging the goals and dreams we set for ourselves. We can be our worst enemy sometimes.

Sarah lived in a time where there were no phones, cars, or running water. Sarah had nothing like anything we have in our times. My encouragement to you is this, when I start feeling like things are not going in my favor I just think that I could have been born in biblical times of in a country that has no freedom.

It is Getting Real

Sisters think about those times and see how you would feel. I personally would not survive because the first time they tell me not to speak: my first words would be why? Or you don't own me!(Laugh)Right then I would be stone to death. It would be over with my generation. Ladies It's something to think about.

The Blessing

We are truly blessed because there is no better country to live in than the US. I'm glad that I'm a black woman, I'm glad I'm free, I'm glad I'm a mother, sister, aunt, grandmother and a great grandmother. It doesn't get any better than this. I get it when God told Sarah she would conceive. Sarah had to give faith So if you can take anything for my story take this, the patient trust God and have faith and you too can carry on the famous tradition of being this greatest mother of all time. Sarah is the mother of all nations. Just as we are the mothers of our families which we hold together. Growing up watching and hearing the women in my family being loved by their husbands was beautiful! That is the reason I'm the woman I am today. Faith is a powerful force and we think because of our imperfection that we do not value or we judge concerts where we live or the kind of car you drive. You know? Sarah had to be pretty special for God to take the time out and announce that she was going to have a baby at 90 years old. (Laugh)I know how she feels. It's like when God tells you that I'm blessing you with a new job and a new home to move in at 60. You get my drift hang if you can hang, no pain no gain.

Sarah's History

The tomb of Sarah is still venerated today Advertising, Sarah lived to be 127 years old and her burial is the first one to be mentioned in the Bible. She is buried in the "cave" of the Patriarchs and traditions say that both Abraham and Sarah (as well as Isaac and Rebekah and Jacob and Leah) are buried there.

A Psalm of David

I praise the Lord, because you rescued me.

You did not let my enemies laugh at me.

Lord, my God, I prayed to you, and you healed me

You lifted me out of the grave; you spared me from going down to the place of the dead.

Sing praises to the Lord, you who belong to him; praise his holy name. His anger last only a moment, but his kindness last for a lifetime

Crying may last for a night, but joy comes in the morning. When I felt safe," I said, I will never fear"

Lord, in your kindness you made my mountain safe. But when you turned away, I was frightened.

I called you, Lord,

and asked you to have mercy on me.

I said, "What good will it be if I die or if I go down to the grave? Dust cannot praise you;

It cannot praise you

it cannot speak about your truth.

Lord, hear me and have mercy on me.

Lord, help me"

You changed my sorrow into dancing.

You took away my clothes of sadness, and clothed me with happiness.

I will sing to you and not be silent.

Lord, my God, I will praise you Forever.

Let the Spirit Work

Now my Lord has an overwhelming and powerful

Spiritual feeling over me. I am so glad that God loved me enough to take so much mercy on me that every time I get into my feelings. I remember the day he saved me from death. Trust me when I tell you that the only being that I trust and love is my father God... he will never leave me nor forsake me. He is the one that can Judge me in this world. He is my Good ole daddy. Meaning GOD. Whenever God tells you that he is blessing you with a gift , believe it. You can bank on it, he is our advisor, doctor, lawyer and best friend. look over your wonderful life and thank him, because of all the women of the world that could have been born he has chosen us. So when God said to Sarah that she would bear a son, he chose her. That's my God your God our God. So, go ahead and step out on faith, god will be the one holding the door waiting for you. Never let anyone take the power from you. Remember God holds the power to the kingdom.

I pray that you are blessed and well. Amen

Laugh at my pain, now laugh at yours!

What is Absent is Present

Latonya Neal

Latonya was born in Abilene, TX and moved to Fort Worth, Texas in 1996 and received her high school diploma through an online accredited school. A few years later went back to school to receive her CNA certification. Latonya was blessed to receive an award in leadership at her Job in Home health. Through the trials and tribulations of separation with her ex-husband. She once lived from place to place hotel to hotel but through prayer and her faith in God. She was blessed with a new home and a new car.

She was blessed to start her own business caring for the elderly. She quoted "I know that I will face more trail's in my life but it brings me comfort knowing that my father in heaven and the holy Spirit is with me, I will continue to allow the holy Spirit to guide me lead and position me to do the will of my father and not my own. I'm ever so grateful to be a part of Sisters of Sarah, may each story touch, reach and bless you." If anyone would like to reach out to Latonya you can email her at 34latonya@gmail.com or find her on Facebook under Latonya Johnson

Let me first start off, by giving praise and honor to our father in heaven. It's because of him I am able to share my story with you. It's also an honor to be able to be part of this amazing book titled: "Sister of Sarah" I pray that my story encourages and inspires whomever may read it and need it. 1st Thessalonians 5:11 says. "Therefore encourage one another and build each other up just as in fact you are doing.

"Absent dad, broken marriage and present father."

Growing up with a learning disability and not having my Earthly father in my life. Was a little hard and very embarrassing, especially when I was in high school. Being told to go down to special ed class, just to take a test was so humiliating. It's not that I wasn't smart or couldn't understand the assignments or tests. I just needed more time to complete the test.

Now, none of my peers made fun of me during those times it was mainly me being hard on myself. Sometimes we can be our own worst critic...Not to mention but when I was 10yrs old I was told by my mom, that my dad, wanted to take me with him, because he didn't want me being dumb like her. So being told that at 10yrs old was heartbreaking, crushing and disturbing. It stuck with me throughout my life so, knowing how my father felt about my mother and him also leaving was very hard for me. It has always bothered me, that I didn't have my earthly father in my life, I would see my two brothers with their fathers. I would get so sad and ask my mom, "where is my dad? "Why doesn't my dad come to see me like my brother's dad's come see them? Never getting the answer of "why, because my mom didn't know the answer herself. Even though I didn't have my earthly father in my life, my mother was a God-fearing, nurturing, loving, giving, relaxed but not easy to get over on. She made sure my two brothers and I had what we needed.

Momma kept us in church even if she couldn't be there due to work, she made sure we were there every Sunday. Proverb's 22:6 Say's "Train up a child in the way he should go and when he is old, he will not depart from it.

"My abilities did not dis me!"

Even though having a learning disability and not having my father around as a child didn't stop me nor discourage me. It actually motivated me, encouraged me and challenged me to do better. During that time, I participated in various high school programs. Such as choir and joining our schools pep squad which I enjoyed participating in and did very well in both. I was also in choir at our church as well. My grades were average but passing. However, I didn't graduate high school. I managed to make it to my 12th grade year. Outside of skipping and hanging out with friends and family. Didn't do me much good, I lost focus. I was having sex, drinking and smoking marijuana. I stopped going to church on a regular basis. I was hanging out, going to teen clubs and house parties. I wanted to be grown. I was rebellious, angry and needed my Earthly father I thought. Whom I don't remember, but still wondered if he were here and How different things would be.

John 3:1 Say's "How great is the love the father has lavished on us, that we should be called children of God!

Think for a minute on the word "Lavished" I took the liberty of looking up the definition: Lavish-1) expended, bestowed, or occurring in profusion: lavish spending.2) using or giving in great amounts; prodigal (often followed by of): lavish of time; lavish of affection. Not having my father in my life, didn't allow me to experience a father daughter bond. Nor allow me to know what it's like to be protected by him, to know what it's like to be Lavished with love, affection, time, correction or provision. Even as a young teenager I learned that God is my Father in heaven, all that I didn't receive from my earthly father I received from my father in heaven. God continued to be my source, my provider, he corrected me when I was wrong, he continued to love me and bless me even when I felt I didn't deserve it.

Psalm 119:105 says: thy word is a lamp unto my feet, and a light unto my path.

When I Moved from Abilene to fort, worth at the age of 19. I decided I needed to start a new life, to get away from things and people that weren't doing me any good. I trusted God to direct my path, to also give me courage, wisdom, guidance and knowledge into my next journey. Not graduating high school didn't stop me from exceeding. I moved to Fort Worth Texas in 1996 to live with my mom's older sister and her husband. I really didn't know what It was that I wanted to do, now that I resided in Fort Worth, Texas. I wasn't attending church during this time. Although, I still loved and depended on God to direct my path. You know the saying, "It's not what you know, it's who you know. That's exactly how I got my first and second job, while living in Fort Worth. My first job was fast food, that job lasted only a few months. Until I landed a much better opportunity working at the hospital, as a Unit Secretary. With better pay and plenty of opportunities to grow. I worked in Labor and Deliver, OB/GYN (Gynecologist unit) and sometimes I would float to NICU (Neonatal unit). Working in the hospital taught me a lot, it was a great experience. I also discovered how much I love helping others. Being in the medical field was new to me, but was definitely what I wanted to pursue more. I continue to work in the hospital, that's where. I met my soon to be ex-husband and oldest daughter's father. We didn't do the traditional marriage then family, I had my first child at the age of 22 and I was married at 24. When I found out that I was pregnant, I couldn't believe it. I thought for years that I couldn't conceive, not that I was ever told that I couldn't. It was because I've had slip ups in past relationships, and nothing happened before then. What I figured out, God had a plan for me, it just wasn't the way I planned it.

"God has the map just follow."

Proverbs 16:9 Says "The heart of man plans his way, but the Lord establishes his steps. Living in a new city married, a great job and a new baby. Seems to me like I made a great move, thanks to my father in heaven. Whom continued to remain in my life. I continued to acknowledge that he was my source know matter where or who I was with. Deuteronomy 31:8 says: it is the Lord who goes before you. He will be with you; he will not leave you or forsake you. Do not fear or be dismayed. I've learned early in life that without having God in my life, it would be easier to give up. Since I was taught about God earlier, I knew that wasn't an option for me. We got married in our 20's trying to raise our first child. We had guidance but not from God in the beginning. In the beginning We tried it our way, trying to figure things out without God. In the relationship it was a constant disaster. From, arguments, fighting, being disrespectful and not getting along! That wasn't the example of life I wanted for my daughter. At first, I started going back to church then we as a couple started going to church together. Things began getting better, we would pray as a family and get more into church. I went back to school to an online accredited school and obtained my High school diploma. At this time, I was no longer working at the hospital but I was still working in the medical field caring for the elderly. Working for a home health service, I loved it so much. I eventually went back to school to become a Certified Nursing Assistant. Only problem was that my marriage didn't quite go as planned. We were young and truly weren't ready to be married. We both came from broken homes, with just one parent to be raised by. Not shown how to be a wife, his husband led us to having a failed marriage. I feel because we didn't start off putting and keeping God first in our relationship, not to mention not having ourselves together. That also played a huge part in the demise of our marriage. I don't want to go into the blame game or point any fingers. As to who dropped the ball, in our marriage. I've learned that I have to take accountability, for my own actions in the part I played. For years I pointed and placed the blame somewhat on him. Because he decided to walk away from the marriage. I was so hurt but not seeing my fault as to why he left. I didn't truly love him the way I should have. I believe he didn't truly love me. With all of the cheating, lying, belittling and being disrespected Made It easy to keep another man in my heart, that I didn't get over from childhood. I tried to get over him by moving away and getting married. It worked at first but somehow, he managed to get into my thoughts. I can remember telling myself that I wasn't going to think about him today. I even told my soon to be ex-husband at one time that I still had love for my childhood friend because I didn't feel he was appreciating me also taking me for granted. I was getting fed up with our relationship after 13yrs of the same repetitive behavior. I think I just wanted a way out to be honest, because nothing was changing between us. I told him that I wasn't in love with my childhood friend, but still loved him obviously because I often thought about him. I was married and in love with my husband. My husband wasn't in love with me and I wasn't the only thing he was thinking about. We stayed together for 13yrs trying to make it work, but not really appreciating one another. We were comfortable and content with how things were. Well I figured this was how it was going to be and I got used to it. No matter how much we prayed or sought counsel from our pastor. Things just never changed between us; our daughter deserved better from us. I didn't want her growing up in a broken home. Like our parents both did. When he finally walked out, I was crushed, hurt, lost and depressed. Leaving me to take care of everything and him not caring about his family's well being, was even more devastating! 1Thessalonians 5:18 says "Give thanks in all circumstances; for this is God's will for you in Christ Jesus." Even during my depression, I prayed and fasted thanking God for giving me the strength to get through each day.

Having godly people around me to help me remember where my help and strength comes from, encourage me to continue on. Even though he walked away I've never held a grudge against him. Him putting me on child support when throughout our marriage I was the breadwinner majority of the time, still no grudge. Speaking badly about me to my child, I still held no grudge. I've never been a person to hold a grudge. God created me to have a forgiving heart so it makes it hard to stay mad at those that wronged me. God wants us to forgive so that he will forgive us. Matthew 6:14 For if you forgive other people when they sin against you, your Heavenly father will also forgive you. I understood that as a child and I continue to live by that scripture in my life today. Jeremiah 29:11 says "For I know the plans I have for you; declares the Lord, plans to prosper and not to harm you. Plans to give you hope and a future." I know now that my soon to be ex-husband wasn't God's plan for me, other than us being Blessed with our daughter. That to me was the only plan for our time together. Let's stop here and reflect on my story a bit. Everything that I've experienced in my marriage was a blessing and a lesson. Blessings because of my beautiful daughter that came from it, that I'm very thankful for a lesson to know what things I ought not do or accept in my next marriage. I know better than to jump into another marriage, without making sure God is the head of the relationship. Making sure the man that calls me his wife loves me like it says in Ephesians 5:25 "For husbands, this means love your wives, just as Christ loved the church, He gave up his life for her. I don't know what plans God has for me on my next marriage, I trust it will be God's will and plan. Writing my story and being somewhat transparent is something I needed to do. I needed to expose my sin so that I can forgive myself and repent of my sins. Hopefully my story can help someone else going through the same thing. Throughout my life I have trusted God to guide me in the direction he is wanting me to go. Through everything, I never lost my love and passion for caring for others. Caring for others I feel is my purpose in life. I get so much joy and happiness being a blessing to others. God has allowed me to care for people that have invented things that we use today. I was Blessed to accompany someone that I cared for on her private jet to Miami, Florida for five days on an all paid trip. I was also gifted a car and money from someone I cared for after their passing. I've also cared for people that couldn't give anything but genuine appreciation for my help to them. I can't walk by a homeless person without giving them something. Understanding that God wants us to be of service to others   James 1:17 says Blessed is the man who remains steadfast under trial, for when he has stood the test, he will receive the crown of life, which God has promised to those who love him. Philippians 4:19 says "And my God will supply every need of yours according to his riches in glory in Christ Jesus. Hebrew 13:16 "Do not neglect to do good and to share what you have, for such sacrifices are pleasing to God. Proverbs 22;9 "Whoever has a bountiful eye will be blessed, for he shares his bread with the poor. The scriptures that I just shared are scriptures of being a Blessed person and doing good to others. No matter what life has thrown at me, I manage to overcome because of God's love, mercy and Grace. I know God loves me because he keeps my mind and heart staying focused on what he created me to do for him. I know God loves me because while I'm a work in Progress, he's still blessing me.

My Journey to Jesus

Nicole Ajibola

I Remember

I grew up in Camden, New Jersey to a family that loved the lord. I Remember my family being sold out for Jesus Christ. I remember events when the lord would show up at times when my mother and aunt only had about seven dollars to their name. I remember the Lord providing food, finances and cars for my family. I remember! Sisters of Sarah journey with me and take a glimpse of my life, these are some of the events that led me to my new Christ filled life and addictions in the past.

My House

My mother had a few family members who lived with us and one was my grandfather, a man I did not like. My grandfather was abusive and so mean. I remember my mother saying my grandmother left him and left all of her kids with him. This led my mother to raise her brother and sisters. At this time my mother was a very young lady never getting to finish school. She was determined to keep her siblings together. Only going to the fifth grade and being the second oldest of 8 children my mother never had a childhood.

Our Secret

During this time my grandfather is living with my mother and he is starting to get older and needed my mother to take care of him. One day while talking to my grandfather i was told "not to ever have sex with a man for free." You probably can imagine the way I felt at such a young age listening to those words come out of his mouth. By the age of 6 my grandfather was already molesting me, this continued until I was 12 years old. At this point in my life my grandfather was making me have sex with his friends for money as well. I did not know then but I know now that he was selling my body. Where I'm from we call this PIMPING, at this very young age my grandfather was teaching me how to become a prostitute. While growing up he would sneak his friends in the house and let them have sex with me. My mother was always at work and after work she would go straight to church, because of that she would not take us with her so that left my grandfather in charge to watch us. As time progressed because of my mother's work schedule, if my grandfather had planned, my mother would allow this neighborhood babysitter to watch me and my siblings. This was a man that watched all the kids in the neighborhood. To be exact he was one of our neighbors. This man would go to the store for everyone and take out their trash. He seemed like a nice man. He gave us cookies, candy and cakes he would even play games with us. Well, I knew it was too good to be true. One day the babysitter took me down to the basement and made me have sex with him. Now I'm being molested by several men!

The Grandfather no one Wanted

I remember a time when this nasty man put his hands on me, we were watching TV with my brother and sisters. After a few minutes my grandfather told me to go into the kitchen. I was scared, I really did not know why I was going in the kitchen. I go into the kitchen and he takes me down to the basement all while the T.V kept my siblings' attention. While in the basement my grandfather started kissing me all over, after abusing me he put his hands around my neck and said to me if I was to say anything to anyone, he would beat me. My grandfather then continued to kiss me all over. As he Proceeded to take my innocence I would scream and he would cover my mouth saying, I better shut up before my siblings hear me and tell someone. I remember my grandfather telling me that Because he was an adult, he was able to do what he wanted. Because I was a child, I had to take it and no one would believe me. As he continued pushing, taking my innocence tears began to run down my face and I heard my aunt bell praying. I was praying with her in my vision and next thing I knew he stopped! After cleaning and wiping himself on me, he said! "get up and put your clothes and take a bath. He said all of this with his hand STILL around my neck, looking me dead in my eyes saying "don't forget what I told you" I was so scared.

I ran up from the basement to my bedroom jump on my bed and began to cry very quietly. My grandfather came upstairs in the room saying "you better not start acting different, you better be the same as you've always been."

The Bathroom Experience

I ran my bath water as I was taking down my underwear, I realized I had blood in my panties and I was hurting so bad. I did not know what to do. "Who do I say" I was scared. I got into the tub I was hurting so bad I just sat in water holding myself because the water was beginning to burn me. All I could do was cry, I just couldn't believe what just happened to me, I really did not understand why he did this to me. Oh, my goodness what I'm I going to do? What did I do to deserve this? Is this some kind of punishment? I was asking myself these questions in the back of my mind. While sitting there I just thought about what my Aunt Bell said to me. She would say, "this man name Jesus will protect you and keep you,"

What just happened then? Why didn't Jesus just protect one? Why did he let this happen to me? what do I do oh my goodness!! I sat in the tub with my legs bent up and holding my knees up to forehead with my head down rocking back and forth crying I felt like everything just left out my body. I did not feel the same anymore, I felt dirty and nasty I began to scrub my body so hard I started bleeding, "it was a bad spirit on me that would not leave my body" I started scrubbing my nose and face until it was so sore and began to bleed as well.

The New Me

I went into my room; I got in my bed and covered up my whole body and head and just cried and cried trying to figure what just happened to me. Now, at this point in my life I'm so confused about life and this man that everyone says is so good. (Jesus) why is he protecting everyone else and not me. All this dancing and thanking Jesus I had questions. Do we only praise him when things are good? What happens when things are going wrong? This is me still under my cover crying and thinking. At this point, sisters, I just wanted to scream!

And then the Door Opened

I heard a door open and noises of laughter" oh no! It is my Mother and Aunt Bell coming, what am I going to do" all in my mind I would ask the question, " I wonder if they know what happened to me?" " will I look different?" As sore as I was, I jumped up, went and washed my face and straightened up. I was hoping that they wouldn't ask for me. I stayed upstairs until I was called down. Finally, my mother asks where I was. My grandmother tells her that I was upstairs sleeping so that bought me a little time to recover. While Upstairs fake sleeping, I was listening to everything that was being said. I was hurt and confused about who God was and what was his purpose to people Especially the ones in my case that are being hurt. Why would they say he comes to save, but yet allows me to be hurt by my grandfather?

Table Talk

My mother cooked dinner That evening and sent my brother upstairs to get me, shaking so bad I really did not know what to do. I went downstairs and sat down but my mother. I believe she saw something different in me. She asked me what was wrong. I was a person that smiled and because I was not smiling, she looked over and asked my grandfather what was wrong with me.

All of a sudden, I felt this big kick from my grandfather, this man reached his leg under the table and kicked me. I jumped! my mother said, "girl what is wrong with you?" I stood up and said "my stomach is hurting, and I'm not feeling good" I was about to throw up, I put my hand over my mouth and ran up stair to the bathroom my Aunt Bell got up and followed me, I was throwing up all over the place. She got a wet rag and put it over my forehead and asked me what was wrong. I told her I was not feeling good she said go lay down and she would check on me later. She gave me a hug and said you don't have a fever, maybe your tummy is upset. " I'm going to make you some soup" I wanted to tell her so badly why I really felt sick but I really did not want to get in trouble, so I just let it go. I just wanted to stay in my room that day my Aunt Bell fed me the soup and said for me to lay down and get some rest, well y'all know the story my mother went to church and work often so that required a babysitter for me and my siblings. For a while my Aunt would stay with us until my mother would come in from work. Things were looking a little better at least for a while, I was much happier around this time but as life happens my mother will continue to go to work and church and leave me at home and because of that this nightmare would happen all over again.

My grandfather had sex with me whenever he wanted, whenever he got ready he did it, this became a part of my life, it was my new normal. I hated the smell of him. It made me sick all the time. There were times when I wanted to put a knife in him, there were so many things I wanted to do to this man. I even thought about pouring gas on him and throwing a match letting him burn up. I was so tired of this man doing this to me, I wanted to tell but I just did not know how.

School Life

I was going through a-lot in school. This boy used to bully me all the time. Again, why is this man named Jesus, the same man my mother and my Aunt Bell and the rest of my family are always praising allowing this to happen. Is it because I'm a kid? I had questions. I always had this stuck in the back of my mind, where is this man everyone is so happy about and why am I not happy about him? At this time, I thought about killing myself, and killing everyone that was hurting me. But I never had the heart to do it, this abuse went from the age of 6 until the age of 12. One day my Aunt Bell was sitting down stairs so I went down there and talked to her. I said Aunt Bell does God like little children. She said well, yes Nikki he loves everyone." "Why are you asking me this question?" she said." "well isn't he watching everyone." Why yes nikki." "well if he is watching us then why do he allow people to get hurt." She said, "honey he doesn't" she asks if someone is hurting you, I said yes! She asks who.

I wanted so badly to tell her about my Grandfather and the Babysitter; I just could not do so. I told her about the little boy that was bullying me at school calling me names and picking on me every day. I told her he makes me cry, I asked her, "why wouldn't God make him stop" and why isn't God protecting me" my Aunt Bell said well honey, God do protect us all the time, she said, this is what I want you to do honey, I want you to get on your knees right now and repeat after me, so I did.

Aunt Bella's Prayer

Father God please hear me. I'm asking you to please protect me and cover me with your precious blood. I know you know what I need. Please help me because I can't help myself, you said in your word that the battles are not mine it yours, vengeance is not mine, it's yours. Dear God, help me fix all these things that's going wrong in my life, help me dear God fix it for me, this boy that's bothering me. Dear God, I want him to leave me alone please help me. In the name of Jesus.

I hugged my Aunt Bell and told her that I loved her so much. Aunt Bell said to me, "anytime you have a problem just talk to God and he will always be there for you no matter what, just talk to him, and he will hear you and fix it for you." "Do you hear me young lady?" I said yes ma'am I will. Aunt Bell Gave me the tools I needed. I ran up the stairs to pray another prayer that I did not want her to hear.

My Personal Prayer

Dear God I'm so tired of my grandfather and what the babysitter is doing to me, can you please make them stop! I'm tired of them messing with me not only him but his friends too God you know the ones that he makes me have sex with for money." Dear God I'm tired please help me, make it stop.

Dear God, do you hear me? I'm on my knees crying and crying and praying so loud.

I was praying so loud that My Aunt bell came up stairs to find what I was praying about. I just kept saying Jesus please help me!!! I'm so tired! My Aunt Bell began to pray with me she never knew what I was praying for but she began to say this *"Dear Father whatever my niece is praying do it for her in the name of Jesus." she told me to just call on Jesus repeatedly and I did. "Jesus, Jesus, Jesus please do it for her, right now she's crying out to you Lord, God I know you are able to fix whatever it is she needs do it for her right now."* I gave my Aunt Bell a big hug and she said I love you baby God is going to answer your prayers just believe it, he will do it in the name of Jesus.

Exposed

One day we all went to church and my pastor asked people to come up to the altar, with me praying in my mind, I was praying for this to stop happening to me, After I went up my mother came up with my brothers and sister then Aunt Bell. My pastor prayed for everyone, she asked my mother and Aunt to stay up there with me, I grabbed my Aunt Bell's hands. The pastor said, to my mother "God has spoken to me about your Daughter he has given me a word for you." I did not know what that all entailed, she asked my mother was her father living with her she said yes, he is, the pastor said well, "you need to get him out of your house because he is touching your Daughter." She said, "this has been going on for a long time, she said, it's time for you to pay attention to your family and get your father out of your house." wow! tears, just came down my face. I did not have to tell. Me as kid, just could not figure out how my pastor knew this information, especially if she never ever lived with us, how did she find out about this?

Mad Mother

Well, my mother was not looking good after this she looked very upset, then I began to worry, I was thinking when I got home, I was going to get in trouble. I started crying, my Aunt Bell said, "Don't you cry this is not your fault-baby; stop crying we are going to talk about this when we get home no worries." Aunt Bell was very upset and so was my mother. My mother seemed to be angrier than my Aunt Bell. well, we go home and my grandfather was not in the house at the time and my mother began to yell," how can this happen, why wasn't I told anything?" My Aunt Bell was telling my mother to calm down and let's get to the bottom of this and get it resolved. Next thing I know my mother was in her room crying throwing things all over the place, my Auntie stayed by my side she took me in my room to talked to me, she ask me "is this why you were crying so hard that day when you were praying" I told her yes, she ask why haven't you told anyone about this, I told her I was afraid to tell, "grandpa said, if I were to tell anyone I was going to be on punishment and I would get in trouble and because he was an adult that you all would believe him and not me." He choked me all the time and told me I was to never tell. With all the spill I decided to tell her about the baby sitter and all the other men grandpa brought into the house to have sex with me. She was in shock. She asked me how long this has been going on. I told her ever since I was six, she could not believe it, she said," how could this have gone on without us even knowing," I told her it happened every time you all left the house. Aunt Bell hugged me and cried, I remember her saying that, she was so sorry that this had happened.

Troubled Mother

Finally, my mother came to my room. She was angry. She had a belt in her hand as my grandfather said, my Aunt Bell jumped up and said to what are you doing? my mother said, "she should have told me." My Aunt Bell pushed my mother to the wall and said to her, "are you crazy? "you are about to beat her for something she had no understanding of? "it was your father who did this to her, it's him you need to beat, she's a child have you lost your mind?" She told my mother to get out of my room and go pray because she has lost her mind. My Aunt Bell grabbed me and said honey no worries you will not get in trouble at all don't you ever in your mind think that you did something wrong because you haven't.

Aunt bell was holding and telling me how much she loved me, I was happy because this was all over for me now the story is out.

The Story is Out

I never understood why my mother was mad at me, so the story got out to the family and to some neighbor concerning my grandfather and the babysitter. What I could not understand was why no one went to jail for what they did to me. Everything was kept quite all my mother did was put my grandfather out of her house nothing else was said about it.

I Started to Believe

I began to believe in this man they called God when I cried to him he answered my prayers, my mother began to treat me different, as I got older I realized that she was an Evangelist in the church and the story about me got out and because of that she was so mad and hurt and embarrassed. The people said, "she was out doing things for the church and for others but neglected her own household and children.

1 Timothy 3:5 says for if a man knows not how to rule his own house, how shall he take care of the church of God. I realized my mother was so much into her own life and others, she forgot all about herself and who she was and that was a mother. My mother neglected her own children to do for others.

My Encouragement to you is this, you can't teach nor help others if you can't take care of your own household, this is a part of my story and life

Later Years

I rebelled at the age of 14 and went to the streets looking for love, looking for the love of my father and mother. I began to make decisions in my life with no guidance, no teaching, no instructions I got on drugs at a very young age. I tried to cover up the hurt and pain. I never could understand why nothing happened to the ones that hurt me. I grew up with hatred towards my mother, it was so much bitterness toward her my life was never the same. she should have been there, she should have protected me, I watched her care for others and give them love, help and information. I never dreamed of becoming a

Drug addict and prostitute. For 20 plus years, I lost my children, my respect, my morals, my women hood, and almost lost my mind throughout my life, by committing suicide 7 times. I wanted to die because I was so lost and so confused about a lot of things. I have so much more to my story I would love to tell, I have 2 books coming out about my life before and after, there is so much more to my life that you must know.

Over the years my life began to come back together, when I surrender and gave my life back to God things started to look better. Although I should have been dead many times god saved me, if it wasn't for him, I would not be here today through his grace and mercy and love god has kept me all these years, because I have a purpose in that is to preach the Gospel and do his will.

Look at Me Now

I am an Evangelist preaching his word thanking God every day for the renewing of my mind, I'm also a business owner looking to expand my business. God said I shall be the head and not the tail, we as his sisters are above and not beneath, we as sisters are the lenders and not the borrowers, Sisters of Sarah I want to say, "don't let the devil steal your life, don't allow your past to consume your future, remember the key to all is our Father, he is the answer to all he is who made all this possible:

2 Corinthians 12:8-10

Three times I pleaded with the Lord to take it away from me. But he said to me, "My grace is sufficient for you, for my power is made perfect in weakness." Therefore, I will boast all the more gladly about my weaknesses, so that Christ's power may rest on me. That is why, for Christ's sake, I delight in weaknesses, in insults, in hardships, in persecutions, in difficulties. For when I am weak, then I am strong. This is one of the scriptures I use to keep my strength, reading the word of God and praying keeps you holding on. Sisters let us not worry because the battles we face are not ours, they belong to the Lord.

Philippians 4:6-7 Be careful for nothing; but in everything by prayer and supplication with thanksgiving let your requests be made known unto God. And the peace of God, which passed all understanding, shall keep your hearts and minds through Christ Jesus. **Proverbs 3:5-6** Trust in the LORD with all thine heart; and lean not unto thine own understanding. In all thy ways acknowledge him, and he shall direct thy paths.

Sisters of Sarah, keep prayer and reading the word of God, keep trusting and watch God direct your path.

Sisters of Sarah

Give Me a Piece of That Peace

Raine D. Fossett, M.A.Ed, CLU

My identity is not defined by my trials but in my trials, I found my identity." - Raine Diane

By profession, Raine is an analyst with one of the top auto insurers in the country for almost 15 years. An analyst by day and creative writer all the time, Raine, has a mission to be a voice of encouragement each day. Love of writing, came from her late aunt Michelle Williams. One of her life missions is to remind people that pain is temporary but their purpose is forever.

Raine has written many poems, motivational quotes, and Bible plans. She continues to branch out in the areas of books, more to come.

Raine holds a Bachelor's degree in Business Administration and Master's Degree in Education, she also holds several insurance designations including Chartered Life Underwriter and her Life/Health license. She has a goal to empower others through her writing and education. She prides herself on being a lifelong learner.

Although, Raine has many credentials the most important thing she wants to be known for is being a Christian. Without Christ she is nothing. Raine resides in North Texas with her 2 children, Mia and Michael. You can find Raine on Instagram and Facebook as RaineRealities

Unrealistic expectations lead to devastation while a

sane mind leads to manifestation – Raine Diane

Whose expectation is it anyway?

As a woman, you are expected to be a one stop shop 24/7. You are expected to have it "all", together, all the time. Your face must be beat with perfect eyebrows, your hair must have every curl in place, your heels should be high, you must wear a never-ending smile, and even then, your teeth need to be pearly white. You are expected to clean the home, put meals on the table, work out, attend meetings, raise the sweet little angels also known as children, volunteer at the school and at the church, be an expert at 4th grade math (don't even get me started here), while simultaneously making career moves. As if that wasn't sufficient, you must be the best at everything, so meeting expectations is not merely enough, you must exceed them!

Are you exhausted from reading this list of expectations? You should be! It is time for some self-reflection, when was the last time you had a "come to Jesus meeting" with yourself to ask "where did these expectations come from?". Were they created based upon someone else's social media profile while scrolling on Instagram, Facebook, or Twitter? Are they based upon the lifestyle of the Real Housewives or was it Basketball Wives? Were they founded upon a different version of you that you think the world would accept more than who you already are? Have you created unrealistic expectations for yourself? Whose expectations are these? Questions that need answers!

Once you have gotten to the root of these expectations, you must determine what to do with them. First things first, pause and remember who you are! Remember who equipped you to be the heartbeat of the home. Remember who called you to be a wife and/or mother, remember who instilled the vision of your goals, remember who you are! Once you have done that, then it is time to recognize that everything you need is already in you, unless it is 4th grade math. God has equipped you with power, love and a sane mind. Don't lose your mind trying to exceed expectations that will not manifest into anything but disappointment.

With all of the competing expectations, it is easy to become overwhelmed, exhausted, and depleted. This leads to unfulfillment and depression, the enemy will plant seeds that you are not enough. This is a lie! If you find yourself in a place of confusion, remember your God is not the author of that. Cast it out!

Expectations are great to have when they come from the right source. So, what is the right source? His word is our guiding tool through life. In His word lies a true measurement of your expectations. Those expectations are to not grow weary in well doing, faint not, let your light so shine, seek ye first the kingdom of God, love your neighbor, forgive 70 x 7, pray without ceasing and do all things for the glory of God. Nowhere does it mention perfection. In fact, God's word reassures you that you will lack nothing, not one thing, instead what is in you will manifest. Someone's healing is based upon what God called you to do, the challenges you survived (did I mention 4th grade math), and every obstacle you have overcome.

Scripture References:

Galatians 6:9-10: Let us not become weary in doing good, for at the proper time we will reap a harvest if we do not give up.

1 Corinthians 10:31; Matthew 5:16; Matthew 6:13; 1 Thessalonians 5:17; Matthew 18:21-22

Let's Pray:

Dear God:

Thank you for this day, it was a day that was not promised to me, thank you for your protection and keeping me safe. I pray that you reveal my purpose, and continue to show me why you favored me. Each day I pray that I have the confidence to accept who I am in you! Increase my peace, finances, and my health. Guide my every step and give me the strength to accept your will even when it doesn't look like I want it to look.

God, please bless America and the world. Touch our world, heal the sick and the diseased, comfort those who are mourning and broken hearted, provide for the homeless and unemployed, rain your favor, love, and forgiveness on the obedient. Thank you for a perfect man dying for an imperfect world. God right now intercede on the enemy plots to kill, steal, and destroy my home, my peace, and my joy. God, I need you and only you because it's you who provides what I need. Remove negativity in all forms, people, places and things. Lord, you're amazing, awesome, and my strength. Please cover us all.

In Jesus name,

Amen

At times we are asking God for a breakthrough, when we are the breakthrough, just break through! – Raine Diane

Just Get Through It!

Have you ever said to yourself, "I am through with this' ' or "I am too through"! Did you know that THROUGH is a part of the process? Ye though I walk THROUGH the valley of death. I can do all things THROUGH Christ. Grace and mercy came THROUGH Jesus Christ. Therefore, you were buried with Him THROUGH baptism. In this life, you are going to go THROUGH things, but it is important that you grow THROUGH what you go THROUGH.

Nothing you face is a surprise to God, if it gained access to you that means God allowed it. Everything is under God's obedience which includes the hard times you face. That very thing that you are praying for God to remove may be what you need to grow THROUGH. After you have gone THROUGH the process you will come out perfect. Let patience have its perfect work in your life and when you are done, you will lack nothing.

Your God is one who cannot and will not lie, His promise says that the righteous will come THROUGH trouble, which means you will come out on the other side, you are not stuck. Even when the challenges you face are self-inflicted, THROUGH the Lord's mercies you are not consumed. Everything you face has a purpose and that purpose may be to bless someone else. Once you overcome, you must free the person tied to your healing. Sometimes this person is a distant observer, other times it is a random person in a grocery store, it could even be someone right under your roof. Of course, the ultimate end result is for you to enter THROUGH the gates of Heaven and for that reason alone, praise Him. The prerequisite to entering those gates is to go THROUGH trials and tribulations.

At times, you may be pleading to God to just make it stop, end this, or at least show Himself in the midst of the trial. But God is always present, He has and will never leave your side. His word confirms that when you pass THROUGH the waters, He will be with you; and when you pass THROUGH the rivers, they will not sweep over you. When you walk THROUGH the fire, you will not be burned; the flames will not set you ablaze.

In the core of growing THROUGH the storm make sure to get out of your own way; get out of your head. Overthinking has never solved a problem, worrying has never provided comfort, being upset never made God come quicker. The most beneficial thing to do is to have faith!

There are times, when you may be fasting and praying, flat out begging for God to send the breakthrough, did you not know that you are the breakthrough, just break THROUGH! If you are wondering how to do that, all you have to do is be still and wait on God; one thing that is consistent in God's word from Genesis to Revelation is that you are to wait on the Lord. Being still and knowing God will handle is progress. You do not always have to be doing something in order to make progress. As it relates to survival, there is no other way in this life but to go and grow THROUGH it. You are a conqueror THROUGH Him! God is never slacked on His promises, He is not subject to time, you are, be patient! In His word it confirms that you will receive the promise of the Spirit THROUGH faith.

Scripture References:

Acts 14:22 "We must through many tribulations enter the kingdom of God."

Lamentations 3:22; John 3:17; John 14:6; Isaiah 43:2; Galatians 3:14

Let's Pray:

Heavenly Father:

I come to you not asking for anything but praising you for everything. Praise is what ignites your power to another level. Praise invites you into our home, hearts, and situation. Praise changes the atmosphere.

I praise you God for being God. I praise you for being all knowing. I praise you for being the most high, God. I praise you for providing my every need. I praise you for your healing hands and the peace over my mind. I praise you for your son, Jesus and the Holy Spirit. I praise you for salvation. I praise you for the stewards over your word. I am forever grateful for my health and strength. I am thankful for your endurance and long-suffering love. I will continue to praise you for delivering me! I praise you for unexpected blessings, for your favor, protection, love, faith and hope!

I am grateful and praise you for just being God! There aren't enough tongues to praise you but I do! Bless your name!

In your son, Jesus name,

Amen

Some relationships are too expensive, nothing is worth your peace! – Raine Diane

Give me a piece of that peace!

In a world where peace is an endangered species, there is no time to waste it on things, people, habits, or anything else that interrupts it. There is one type of peace that will always exist, the kind that surpasses all understanding. This peace is like none other, it is God given. PEACE! You can't buy it, you can't steal it, you can't earn it, you must trust God and all that He is doing and once you do that, waa-lah, the peace of God becomes yours. It becomes yours because you have cast your cares instead of carrying them.

If you focus on the long-term outcome, you disrupt your peace. If you focus on "why" and not "who", you interrupt your peace. If you wake up early worrying and go to bed worrying, you interrupt your peace. If you let your heart be troubled, you interrupt your peace. If you pray and then doubt, you interrupt your peace. If your burden is heavy it is not meant for you to carry it is meant for you to cast, you can't grasp peace if your hands are full of worry. Sometimes the person interrupting your peace is not the enemy, it is the "inner me". What you internalize becomes your center, if your center is not God, you will be unbalanced and your peace will be disturbed.

Peace is something you have to accept; a layer of accepting peace is trusting in God. When you trust in God it means you are willing to be vulnerable to His will, you trust that His outcome is better than what you want. You trust that His timing is better than your impatience for things to happen. You trust that during the test, His presence is there and you are not alone. This is accepting His peace, additionally trusting in God means that you are in His word, in His presence, in His will, and in prayer!

There are seasons in your life where you will have to seek peace. Seek it until you find it. Work will drive you nuts, seek peace! Marriage goes through peaks and valleys, seeking peace! Children will do the opposite of what you have instilled in them, seek peace! Relationships become strained, seek peace! Bills come faster than money is earned, seek peace! Health issues knock at the door, seek peace! Self-esteem takes a hit, seek peace! Seek it until you find it and when you find it, hang on to it. Share it when you can but don't lose it and definitely do not let anyone steal it.

God's promise to you is that you can cast your cares on Him, that you can take his yoke for it is easy and His burden is light. Another promise to you is that He will give you sleep and it will be sweet. It is also important that you do not surround yourself around turmoil. You must live in peace with everyone, sometimes your peace is interrupted when you withhold forgiveness, when you choose grudges over grace, these are seeds that bloom into bitterness, anger, and aggression. Where is the peace in that?

Do yourself a favor and know God will provide you the peace that surpasses all understanding. So much peace that even your enemies have to be at peace with you! Moral to the story, peace is accepted, it is sought after, and it sowed. No one can steal your peace; you can share it but no one is allowed to steal it or destroy it. If this occurs, abort mission! Anything that disturbs your peace is too expensive.

Scripture References: ·

Philippians 4:7 "And the peace of God, which transcends all understanding, will guard your hearts and your minds in Christ Jesus."

Psalm 34:14; Matt 11: 28-30; 1 Peter 5:7; Proverbs 3:24; 1 Peter 3:11

Let's Pray:

Dear God:

Be with all the people laying in bed overthinking, some are tossing and turning and worrying! Be with those who are battling something in silence. Walk a little closer with those who have many challenges ahead. Touch those who need and want love but reject it, be with those who are just barely hanging on. Comfort those who isolate themselves, send someone into their path right now, increase their peace of mind, and their faith in you! Increase the finances of those who need you more in that capacity, give them the strength and endurance to surrender all to you. God, please make their pain temporary and their blessings everlasting. May the memories of loved ones who have transitioned into your presence bring laughter and smiles. Give us the peace that all things work together for good knowing you've ordered every one of their steps. God, I am trusting in you in all seasons knowing that nothing catches you by surprise. Wrap your arms around our loved ones and be an extra layer of protection. Be with our country as a whole. God you've got the whole world in your hands!

In Jesus name, Amen

Pray without ceasing, believe without overthinking, love without expecting, serve without complaining, forgive without remembering. – Raine Diane

Lost: Still a location on God's GPS!

Have you ever been in a place where you didn't know when or how you got there, you don't know how long you will be there, all you know is that you don't belong in this place! It is the place called "lost", lost is still a destination located in God's GPS. It is a place where you learn a lot about yourself but even more about who God is. Lost is one of the most visited places in the world, you don't need a lot of money to get there, you don't need a passport, you don't need reservations, all you have to do is live! Although it is not the most extravagant place to be, it is a place where many people leave with qualities that change them for the better.

Sometimes you may end up lost at the negligence of others, on occasions you may end up there because of past mistakes or flat out bad decisions. There are times in your life when you visit the land of the lost at not choice of your own but solely because God allowed it, it sucks. On the flip side, you may end up here because you have wandered off from the Lord, you have gone astray, even when this is the cause of your visit, you are still in a place where God can find you. You may be visiting this place right now and all you want to do is get to the other side of it. Instead of pouting because you didn't ask to be here, being upset because you can't snap your fingers and be home, pause and recognize there's a lesson in this! The lesson will make you a better you but the ultimate reward is the benefit it brings to the person watching you from afar or the stranger you will need to minister to years later.

How many times have you asked Jesus to take the wheel but then wanted to control the destination? When you let go of control and trust that God has you exactly where you need to be, you will find peace wherever you are. Now that you have changed your mindset about the location, what do you do while in the land of lost? Pray! Believe! Love! Forgive! Serve! But how?!?!

Prayer is one of the most powerful tools that you have, when you are lost or feeling like you don't know what to do next, pray! Pray without ceasing, you have to get out of your normal prayer cycle which includes good morning prayers, grace, and good night prayers. God wants to hear from you at all times, make your requests known but thank Him as well. If you can't be honest with anyone else, be honest with God. He already knows your most intimate thoughts but there is power in confessing them to your Heavenly Father! Praying without ceasing means to pray whenever and wherever.

There is a misconception about prayer, maybe that is why some people do not do it often, they don't know how. Prayers do not have to be fancy, they do not have to have a long introduction, you do not have to use big words, all it needs to contain is a sincere heart and belief that God is going to answer you. The moment that your prayer includes doubt is the same moment your prayers may not be answered, His word says that those who doubt should not expect anything from Him. When you pray, believe! Come boldly to His throne, decree and declare that it is so, and guess what, IT IS SO! What do you pray when you do not know what to say? Pray His word, it won't return void. Pray all the scriptures you know, replace your name in places where you can and it becomes your own. Now believe and be patient, God doesn't always answer prayers at the end of you saying "Amen", sometimes there is a waiting season.

You are never completely lost; God always has His hands on you. You may feel lost because you do not know your next destination, but God has the roadmap and He has the plans to prosper you, not hurt you. To prosper you, you may have to lose yourself in order to find out who you really are. Trials and challenges build your character and you come out lacking nothing, not one thing! Are you really lost or are you in place of growing and it feels like you are lost because you don't have control? Take pride in knowing that you are always in a place where God can find you, while waiting, find yourself.

Scripture References:

Luke 15: 4-5: "What man of you, having a hundred sheep, if he loses one of them, does not leave the ninety-nine in the wilderness, and go after the one which is lost until he finds it? And when he has found it, he lays it on his shoulders, rejoicing."

Jeremiah 29:11; 1 Thessalonians 5:17; James 1:6-8

Let's Pray:

Dear God in Heaven:

There are times when I feel lost, please remind me you are there. I feel lost when I know the plans that I had for my life and then it doesn't go my way, I just don't know what to do next. God, make your presence known in these moments. Silence the thoughts of doubt and confusion, I know that you are always in the midst. You have plans that will prosper me, Lord, just give me, me! Hold me close and guide me every step of the way, I need you more when I can't find my way. Your son, Jesus said He is the way, the truth and the life, so God, I will always follow Him.

In Jesus name, Amen

There is freedom in forgiveness, hanging on to the

offense is too expensive. I can't afford it. – Raine Diane

Lost: There are lessons that can only be learned in the land of lost. Part Two

One of the most intimidating feelings a person can experience is feeling lost, then throwing in the lack of control. This equals a waiting season. Waiting season, whew, what a scary combination of words. Who wants to wait? No one, but sometimes it's best. If you are in a waiting season, there is plenty to do. The attitude that you have during this season will determine how your faith sustains during the process. It is important that you are waiting with an attitude of service. Wait as you wait!

As you serve it is vital that you do it without murmuring and complaining, God loves a cheerful giver. Your service is not solely referring to monetary gifts, it includes time, talent, material blessings and abilities. Whatever you do, do it as unto the Lord. Remember that you may be entertaining angels unaware, would you want to serve them grudgingly or with complaining? What value does it add when you fuss, complain, pout, become bitter, envious, or jealous during the process of waiting or serving others? The answer is, there is no value, instead you are sowing seeds that will manifest into depression, anger, rage, and impatience. Additionally, when you serve, do it without telling the world what you did. The one who needs to see it will, you do not need the world to validate your acts of service, let God reward you.

While waiting, praying and serving it is imperative that you love and forgive. A part of the waiting season in the land of the lost is to grow, but what if the lack of forgiveness is hindering your progress? God forgives daily, He starts each morning with new grace and mercy. In this life people will hurt you, betray your trust, intentionally neglect you, lie on you, mock you and the list goes on but you must forgive. Forgiveness is a commandment but its reward is freedom, free yourself from remembering the offense. Constantly replaying what happened to you will not heal you, it will delay your progress and it leads to you wanting to take matters in your hands. Your God is a God who will right all wrongs, just stay out the way. God's punishment is far more memorable than anything you can do and why would you need to seek revenge when God says "vengeance is mine!" This does not give you approval to wish God's punishment on anyone, it just means, get out the way and allow Him to handle!

The art of forgiveness needs to also be applied inward, the greatest enemy at times lives within. You may have made mistakes, forgive yourself. You may have hurt someone you love, forgive yourself. You may have not loved yourself enough, forgive yourself. You may not have accomplished all your goals, extend grace and forgive yourself. Whatever it is that you are punishing yourself for, today is the day you forgive yourself. Wipe the slate clean, love does not keep record of wrongs. There are health benefits to extending forgiveness. If you do not consider forgiving your offender and/or yourself you open the door to health concerns. Yes, lack of forgiveness can invite illness. Some of those illnesses may include anxiety, blood pressure concerns, heart disease, and even cancer. This by no means is saying that those who have these illnesses have it because of the lack of forgiveness. It is only a warning that it can bring on physical and mental illnesses. Free yourself from carrying a burden not meant for you to carry! Jesus already carried it to the cross.

Love a four-letter word that carries a lot of weight. It carried a perfect man to Calvary to die for an imperfect world, all because of His love. What does love have to do with it? It was in being lost. It is a life characteristic that you must maintain until God calls you home. You can't be selective with your love because Jesus was not selective with His. You are called to be Christ like which means to love all people as He does. Even when you do not receive the same love in return, love without expecting anything in return. It is easy to love others when they love you, but how you love those who do not love you back is the strength of God. Once you master that, can you love those whom you have deemed unlovable? Those are the people who need the most love. Love helps you find out who you are in Him!

His word says that love covers a multitude of sins. Have you extended this love to the person who hurt you? It is possible that they are the reason why you ended up lost in the first place. What if the key to getting to the other side of loss is to simply love the person past their offense? Can you do that? Of course, you can because you are well equipped with everything you need to be successful which is power, LOVE, and a sound mind! If you are wondering how you forgive others? Love! How do you forgive yourself? Love! How do you pray without ceasing? Knowing the love of God! Perhaps you are the person who has no problem loving others, maybe the struggle is loving yourself. Love yourself because you are worthy of the love that you give so many other people. The love that you freely give to everyone else should be retained for you too, if you give all of yourself, you will end up empty. Furthermore, it is time to let that self-rejection go, love you. You are not perfect nor were you called to be. You will make mistakes and learn from them but never stop loving yourself. There is no one who can love you better than you outside of God.

Scripture References:

Psalm 27:14 "Wait on the Lord; Be of good courage,

And He shall strengthen your heart; Wait, I say, on the Lord!"

Philippians 2:14; Mark 11:25; 1 Peter 4:8; Hebrews 13:2; 2 Timothy 1:7; Romans 12:19

Satan is persistent but God is consistent, my faith is resilient, my goals will soon be in existence. – Raine Diane

RE-Do: I am ready to receive!

Are you ready for a redo? Are you really ready to receive all that God has for you? Are you ready to renounce your old way of thinking? Tell the Lord YES, you are ready to receive whatever it is He has for you. When you speak those things, this means an ultimate surrender of what you had in mind. You cheat yourself when you want to control the outcome, God may have something you never imagined in store. He is a God who will do exceedingly and abundantly more than you could ever think of. Maybe you've been praying for God to revive, restore, and reconcile some things in your life and He hasn't answered those prayers in a fashion that you would like to have seen them answered. Or is it possible that you are still waiting to hear from him? Hang tight, God is not slacking on His promises. He is not a forgetful God. More importantly, He is not a God who will give you something that's incomplete or premature (babies are the exception), so what does this mean? It means that the answer to your prayers are in the faith that you possess. Is your faith equipped to sustain the waiting season?

Sometimes you have to allow the removal of negative people, places, and things. How can God do a new thing in you, if you have not removed the things that hinder you? You must readjust the broken pieces in your life, yes, the pain is real but it's nothing compared to the blessings that will be revealed. All the trials and triumphs are for a valid reason. The catch to this is you may not always know the reason. The reason is sometimes a lesson to bless you, it is sometimes the mechanism to birth your purpose, it could be so that you can free the person who is attached to your healing, or it could be a combination of it all.

God knows that you are not perfect, He never called those who were perfect, there was only one who fit that description, Jesus! With that being said its ok to not be perfect, you will mess up, but thank God for His avenue of repentance. God will refill your cup with daily grace and mercy. This same cup will runneth over with blessings, are you ready to receive? In various seasons of life, you may feel like you need certain people and relationships to continue you on, but you will learn that the only relationship you need is God. Trust that He will direct your path and send you all the people and things you need to survive.

Each day is a gift, it is not something to take for granted. It is not something you have earned or deserved but solely given to you because there is a purpose for your life. Refocusing on you as God reforms your life to be used to help others will rescue you from the thoughts of not being enough. You are in fact more than enough; you were to die for. What a refreshing feeling it is to renew your mind daily and being reminded of how great you are because of how great God is!

Are you ready to receive? Are you ready for the Lord's renovation in your life? Receive it!

Scripture References:

Ephesians 3:20 "Now to Him who is able to do exceedingly abundantly above all that we ask or think, according to the power that works in us,"

2 Peter 3:9; Hebrews 11:1; Isaiah 43:19; Proverbs 3:6

Let's Pray:

Dear Awesome Father:

Lord, I am ready to receive! But importantly Lord, I am ready to serve. Thank you, God, for your word, for in it lies the tools that I need to renew my mind daily.

It is by the renewing of my mind that I am able to receive. Each day you revive me and grant new grace and mercies that I am thankful for because they are not earned or deserved but given because of your love. I refuse to accept the enemy's plots against my life in the form of thoughts and challenges, God I accept you will and your way. Thank you. God for the avenue of repentance and your never-failing love. I am ready to live the life you have called me to live, I am ready to walk in the nature of my calling, I am ready God, send me.

In Jesus name, Amen

May not look good, may not feel good, may not sound good, but all things work together for good! – Raine Diane

With God, I can!

You may have days where you need an extra push, a little encouragement, or someone to believe in you. There are days where you have officially arrived at the stop sign of "Can't do this anymore and I'm over it all." While you are there you begin to speak to yourself things that are not true such as "I can't take this! I can't do this anymore!" You are not alone in this; everyone comes to this place whether they admit it or not. Thankfully, God knows your breaking point, in fact, it is a commandment to the believer to come to

Him all who are heavy laden and He will give you rest. If you choose not to take God up on this offer, there is no one to blame but the one who chooses to carry the load, you!

God is one who cannot lie, He will not put more on you that you can handle, when it becomes unbearable you should cast the load and not carry it. The truth is you may not want to do this anymore because it isn't easy, it's frustrating, it's hard, it's painful, and frankly you've tried to do your way it didn't work. You may want the trial over but God instead is increasing your strength to face the trial.

Each morning recite to yourself, Philippians 4:13, "I can do all things through Christ who strengthens me." After reciting this feel empowered to remove the following words from your vocabulary, "can't, hard, and quit"! Take some time to break down the scripture word for word so that you can receive the power in it. The word "all" encompasses everything, it doesn't exclude anything, even the secrets struggles and the silent cries. "All" includes the very thing that you said you can't get through. You must first be aligned with Him in order to go "through" Him. Through Him suggests that you surrender your control of the situation to God. If it is still in your hands it isn't in God's, let go.

There are times when you do not know what to pray

and there is nothing wrong with that, your Savior, Jesus intercedes as He sits on the right hand of God, so essence, you go through Him in prayer as well. "Strengthen me" suggests there will be times where your spirit and flesh may get weak but you will be armed with the strength to continue to endure. Be confined in His word which says to endure hardship like a good soldier so that he may please Him who enlisted him as a soldier. When you are weak, God is still strong, His grace is sufficient for thee. Don't doubt yourself, but more importantly don't doubt your faith in Jesus Christ and His father, He will make sure you don't fail instead you will prevail!

WITH GOD YOU WILL NOT FAIL! Repeat this to yourself until you believe it even when it doesn't look good. Believe this even when it does sound good to your ears or isn't seen clearly with your eyes. In these moments when your troubles outweighs your faith remember that "all" things includes health issues, relationship struggles, wayward spouses and kids, finances, education goals, health and fitness goals, unemployment, struggles at work, struggles at church, forgiveness, anger issues, addictions, raising kids, using your God given talents, mourning loved ones, watching a loved one diminish, teaching the lost, ALL THINGS THROUGH CHRIST CAN BE DONE! The one requirement is that you must go through Him!

Scripture References:

Philippians 4:13 I can do all things through Christ who strengthens me.

Matthew 19:26; 2 Corinthians 12:10; Romans 8:28; 2 Timothy 2:3-4

Let's Pray:

Dear Amazing Father:

Thank you for this for it is a gift from you! Thank you for the many things I've taken for granted like my 5 senses, jobs, families, and a sane mind. God, I decree and declare that all generational curses are destroyed, all negativity is removed, all past mistakes are learned lessons. I pray that all hurt is healed, the offenders are forgiven, all illness is healed with your touch, all marriages are mended and built upon you. I decree and declare that children are loved and family is appreciated. Be the reconciliation that we all need so that family works out their differences and remember that love covers a multitude of sins.

If you have allowed a void in my life, may it be fill with you so that I as your child don't self-medicate with sex, false relationships, drugs/alcohol, bitterness, shopping or even physical harm.

Bless those who diligently seek you, bless our homes,

our job, finances, and goals. Touch the new babies, new marriages, new engagements, and new opportunities. I can do all things through you! It is done, send me God.

In Jesus name,

Amen

Silent Cries by Raine Diane

Alone hiding in a place with the no one around,

My heartaches and it pounds but I dare not make a sound.

Tears roll with a never-ending stream,

Rocking myself like a newborn wanting to wake up out this bad dream.

I can't let anyone know I'm in this much pain,

Ha! The secret will be out that I am not as strong as I proclaim.

My long nights overlap and become long days,

But I mask it well and no one can tell that my emotions are lost as if they are in a maze.

Sisters of Sarah

Silent cries are the loudest pleas for attention,

The outward expression is not a true reflection of the internal tension.

Without a word I'm screaming,

Constantly to the Lord I am pleading,

Since no one hears no one knows of the burden I carry alone,

The burden of loneliness, rejection, and fear but to the human eye they remain unknown.

Silently I cry out for help but don't know how to let go,

So, until then I let the silent tears flow.

I must not show that I am weak,

So, of these silent cries I cannot speak.

Weeping silently to God for strength to maintain,

My faith in Him is how I sustain.

Speechlessly I refrain,

Refrain from reciprocating hurt to those who willing

brought and watched my pain.

I go to my place of refuge to cry in silent with no shame,

Afterwards I reappear as if nothing happened, this is how I play the game

Silent cries aren't silent at all,

For they are the loudest cry before one falls.

Behind the silent cry is the most pain,

One that only the heart knows but is not understood by the brain.

His Word says weeping may endure for a night,

But I don't put a deadline on God, I just trust that all wrongs will be made right.

I've sobbed in silence for so long that there are no more tears,

Right on the other side of this moment I can see the vision a little clearer.

Silent cries become distant memories in due time,

In due time my desires and God's will begin to align.

Sisters of Sarah

My silent cries become outward praise

My outward praise ignites my faith to walk and trust that His ways are not my ways.

All those silent cries were for my healing,

While I was crying and kneeling, weeping and dealing.

Wiping tears and staring past the ceiling,

My God was removing the hurt while concealing.

Concealing me from pain unseen,

The cries where there were no tears was when Jesus had intervened.

He brought me close and whispered trust me,

Didn't I tell you to resist Satan and he will flee.

He whispered again come to me my burden is light,

All those silent cries when you felt alone, I was there all day and all night.

So, your silent cries were heard amongst the most powerful ears,

Each night it was my strength that made your fears

disappear.

Silent cries I hear them all,

When you couldn't walk, I carried you until you stood tall.

Patience, my child, I felt your pain,

I heard every prayer you called in my name.

Now you are free,

But only because you finally let go and put your trust in me.

Peace be still, keep calm my dear,

Listen silently, I will never leave or forsake you feel my presence, I am always here.

Sisters of Sarah

I Woke Up Different

Ronnycia Mays

One day she woke up different. Even the way her foot hit the floor. The way her first thought came about, the way she looked in the mirror, she was me.

Born and raised in Dallas/ Fort Worth, TX. I grew up in a two-parent home with a younger sister. Mom and Dad both had full-time jobs. Dad worked early mornings, literally the very early morning when it begins to get light. And my mother worked the graveyard shift. So, most of the time we would let mom sleep so she could cook supper and wait on dad to return home to help us with homework. I am now 30 years of age with 3 children, all Boys. My oldest son is 14 years old, his name is Ra'Lon. I conceived him at a very young age, so I'm overprotective of his decisions, wanting his future better than mine. He likes to get dressed for no reason at all, he uses the word "fly." Honestly, I think it's cute. He dreams of being a professional football player and wants to take care of his brothers and I when he gets older. My second child is Antwon Jr. He's 11 and has a very free spirit. Love sports and hanging out with friends. He's my lazy child, especially when it comes to unloading groceries. Then I have to be honest with my two-year-old. He's the most intelligent baby I've ever met. He loves challenges and to be outdoors. Being me was never easy.

Growing Everyday

I'm so misunderstood in many situations. Most of the time I'm just in my thoughts, physically I'm there but my mind is elsewhere. Apparently, I come off to others as sad or even angry while in my thoughts. My Friends would describe me as a sweet person, confused and goofy, not to mention grumpy. I think of myself as Different., I'm a deep thinker. Growing up I always felt different like there were some people who could see through me and feel that I was not like other people.

As I got older, I learned the saying "many are called but few are chosen." Matthew 22:14. Which now as an adult I feel like it's a blessing and a curse at the same time. Something that is both beneficial and a burden. My blessing is sometimes I feel out of my body, a natural high and I can often see the Unseen and feel People's Energy, so anytime I feel a negative vibe I tried to change it. often times people will be going through so much and want to give up and through the grace of God I'm able to help those individuals and they feel better for a moment or two and come back if I am needed again. The downside of it is that I take people's feelings way too serious and it sometimes corrupt my spirit if I'm not able to succeed in helping in any kind of way. Allow me to elaborate.

I attract hurt people with Broken Spirits or damaged thoughts.

I'm still unsure why I feel so chosen when at times I need the person I'm trying to become.

So, I started getting in-tuned with myself more and more, day after day I found something new. I even started to notice my flaws. The biggest one was making excuses, and I'm a huge procrastinator. I'm also very indecisive even over little things. I play the game in my head Eeny, meeny, miny, moe. sometimes I even do it out loud. And yes, I've been working on that, but it won't happen overnight. I often beat myself up because of it. because I realize that I'm a mother and I'm aware that I am my children's first teacher.

No More Excuses

Anyhow, I'll tell you how I had to stop making excuses for myself. For example, I would say to myself I'm getting too old to try and start a business or I'm too tired or sleepy to even function correctly at the moment to do anything. That did no good for me while trying to follow or live my dream. Speaking of dreams, I had so many I started to get sick of myself. No seriously, I always liked myself so it was a big deal and I knew I had to change it. I noticed the excuses were getting easier. And my sleep was getting longer. I've always wanted a nice spacious home with a guest room in a large backyard. I know that I want to become a business owner and I want a clothing line any eventual a whole cosmetic line.

I'm Determined

Now Yes! of course I was physically tired from being a single mom of three children and working overnight to provide for my family. But I was also mentally tired. Due to my visions being unclear because while my school-age children are away at school I'm at home with my toddler because daycare is not in my budget at the moment. So, a lot of the time I don't get the proper rest. On my off days I'm usually sleepy or cleaning or trying to make up time with my family. My children do not agree with my work schedule. They strongly dislike it because I'm always too tired to do extra stuff. So, they always mention how they can't wait until I am blessed with a better job. Unaware of how awful that makes me feel. I'm the thinker for many of my loved ones. So, chasing my dream isn't easy at all. But I have made up my mind to keep pushing through.

My 2020 Vision

If being successful was not enough to motivate me then who I wanted to be successful for was now my motivation. I realize that it was my story to tell.

So, let me tell you how in just a simple mind change, changed everything for me.

I've learned that being happy was my responsibility. And from that day forward being happy is just what I wanted. It wasn't the amount of money in my pockets nor was it the car I drive. I started being happy because I still had life inside in my body, good health and a stable mind. Now I Just wanted to make my children happy and feed them. The simple things. A changed mine, nothing more powerful.

One day I started to write down my goals, big and small. And I witness them manifest. So, in result of that I was surely blown away! I've always had people tell me, "you need to write that down!" And I would agree but never apply. But whoa!, let me tell you, WRITE IT DOWN. Create a vision board! I called this Smart Goal

S.M.A.R.T GOALS

S specific- what do you want to do?

M Measurable- how will you know when you've reached it?

A Achievable- is it in your power to accomplish?

R Realistic- can you realistically achieve it?

T Timely- when exactly do you want to accomplish it?

I've discovered goals give you a starting point and a destination to reach. By not writing down your goals you will find yourself distracted, unmotivated, pierce, and off- course.

It's real. And if you haven't started to take the time to write your goals down don't beat yourself up about it. it's usual for us. It all basically comes down to awareness of who you are and knowing what you want. I knew that I wanted to help others in any way that I possibly could. Even if it was just words of encouragement that's what I wanted to do. I want to help young women like myself heal from broken hearts, encourage people to give themselves another chance at whatever it is they desire. Motivating my family and friends also teaches my son how to be a great man. I'm currently doing something that I love and enjoy with a passion but only part-time.

CEO

I'm now a certified lash technician with the vision of making my own cosmetic line. So every day I tried to at least do one thing worse that go even if all I do is research. I'm often disrupted due to being a single mom and trying to always put my children's needs before my own. So I've taken the time to have a discussion with them about what owning a business is and the sacrifices that come with it. Especially since my older two are always asking me for money and even memorized my payday. Not to mention my youngest child requires a lot of my attention he's growing so fast and I don't want to miss a Beat. So it momentarily impacts me tremendously because sometimes I battle with scheduling time for myself and my goals with time with my family. Occasionally I get to do both but when I'm unable to do so my oldest are great help and they don't hesitate to give me that time. Another one of my favorite quotes is "it takes a village to raise a child." Ecclesiastes 4:9 two are better than one because they have a good reward for their toil. It interprets that two or more, who live together in any kind of society and join their powers together in pursuit of any important object are better than one. I have a really awesome support system my mom sister and their dads are very much active in their lives and I'm forever grateful for that. I also have this astonishing cousin who is always one phone call away. With pursuing my dreams if I could help anyone I will tell them never give up and know that in God's timing you should have any and everything you worked for in to stay prayed up. That you will lose people that you thought would have visions like yourself but some of those people are only there to distract you and it will hurt because you'll come to realize those people can't go where you're going. Learn yourself and love yourself. Believe in yourself and keep God first.

Words Do Hurt

Sherica Thompson

Prayer and Introduction

Let the words of my mouth and the meditation of my heart be acceptable in Your sight, O Lord, my strength and my Redeemer (Psalms 19:14.) Hello, sisters of Sarah. I come to you with a mind filled with a word from God, a heart full of love, and a soul that has been saved by our Lord and Savior Jesus Christ. In Romans 10:13 it says, "whoever calls on the name of the Lord shall be saved." And last but not least I come to you with The Spirit of the living God, which is The Holy Spirit.

Words Do Hurt

Sisters, we go through so many different things in our lives that impact us on a daily basis. One of the biggest things is the words of other people. I would like to talk to you about how words hurt. There are ways we can avoid carrying these hurtful words with us throughout our day and life. Of course, the best way is to give these words and emotions that come with them over to God through prayer. We will discuss more examples later on in the book. Words, among other things, are seeds that can be planted within us. What we must understand is that these words can only be planted within us if we allow them to be. As women we tend to focus on other people's opinions of us. We say that we don't care or as we like to call it "being unbothered." But if we are honest with ourselves, we are very bothered. What people say and think about us interferes with our own thoughts and feeling of ourselves. God created us as emotional beings. We are much more in tune with our emotions and thoughts than a lot of men. It's not just the emotions and thoughts that we have of ourselves, but the ones that people have towards us. As a matter of fact we don't even have to know them personally in order to be impacted by what they say or think about us. The words of family, friends, or even a spouse aren't the only ones that affect us. It can be a co-worker at a new job that you just started or a neighbor that you've never been introduced to. Most of the time, as women, we feel or believe that we are very confident in ourselves. It can be anything from the way we look, to the texture or length of our hair. Maybe it's our skin color, facial features, height and weight, or even the shape of our bodies. But all it takes is one person to come along and say something that will have us second guessing the confidence we thought we once had.

Reflecting Moment: I want you to take some time out right now and reflect on a situation where someone said something to you that was hurtful. This might be something from the past that you still haven't been able to get over. It can also be something from the present time, like a week or a month ago, that hurts your feelings every time you think about what was said. Even though you tried to deal with it from an "unbothered" mindset it had an impact on you. In what way did those words affect you? How did you deal with the impact that those words had on you? Did those words change your entire mind about how you felt about yourself? Did you hold all of your pain and sadness on the inside? What about a projection stand point? Did you push your pain off on someone else who didn't cause this pain by being mean and negative towards them? Ladies, it's ok to admit that words...do...hurt. Job 19:2 says, "How long will you torment my soul, And break me in pieces with your words?" Things like words affect us as long as we hold on to them. Sisters....it's time to release them. Give those words and the people who said them over to God.

Rooftop Access: Access Granted

There will always be people around who have something negative to say. But I want you to ask yourself a question. Do they have rooftop access? Allow me to explain. This actually means exactly what it says, access to the top. Well, what is at the top? Heaven is. Who is at the top? Our Father, God. This is from a spiritual mindset. Now let's ask these same questions from a carnal mindset. What is at the top? It's our emotions, mind, thought processes, and other things that are directly connected to us. Who is at the top? We are always at the top because these are our emotions, mind, and thought processes. Spiritually, can we all have access to God or this rooftop access? Yes, we all can have access and at any time. Let's talk about the things that would keep us from having constant and direct access from the rooftop or God. Whether people want to admit it or not there are things that keep us on a lower level of our relationship with Christ versus being on the highest level with Him. Some of these things include the willingness to sin, holding on to anger, being judgmental, unforgiveness, bitterness, being hateful, negative, and so many other things that go against God.

Scriptural Moment: 1 John 1:5-7 This is the message which we have from Him and declare to you, that God is light and in Him is no darkness at all, If we say that we have fellowship with Him, and walk in darkness, we lie and do not practice the truth. But if we walk in the light as He is in the light, we have fellowship with one another, and the blood of Jesus Christ His Son cleanses us from all sin.

Those of us who truly have rooftop access or a true fellowship with Christ do not indulge in these things. Instead, when we are confronted with the things that are against God, we take them to Him and leave them with Him. In Romans 12:21 His word says, "Do not be overcome by evil, but overcome evil with good."

Reflecting Moment: Sisters what are some things that you are indulging in or holding on to that could interfere with your access being granted? Who and what are you allowing to have or gain access to your emotions, life, heart, mind, or environment? Who are the people that you are holding on to that you know deep down, you should let go of? Ask yourself why you are holding on to them. Are these people less of a helper and more of a hindrance? In Genesis 24:56 it reads And he said to them, "Do not hinder me, since the Lord has prospered my way; send me away so that I may go to my master." Stop allowing people and things to be a hindrance in your life. God has already made your path prosperous. Send those who hinder you away and continue on the path that leads to our Father.

Bulldozer or Builder: You Be The Judge

Some people can be a bulldozer or a builder in your life. In other words, the positive things that you are trying to manifest in your life, how are they contributing to those things? Are they coming around you like a big machine of destruction knocking everything down? I want us to marinate on the meaning of the word bulldozer. I took the liberty of researching the word so that we could get a better understanding of what it means. The word originated in 1876. It's meaning was one who is intimidated by violence. In 1930, the definition was a powerful tractor with a broad upright blade at the front for clearing the ground. The word today is also used as a person or group exercising irresistible power, especially in disposing of obstacles or opposition.

After reading these definitions I was able to realize that I have had plenty of bulldozers in my life at one time or another. I want you to think about whether or not you had or have some in your life. Is there someone that you have granted access to your mind, life, emotions, or environment who tries to intimidate you with violence? Are they the powerful tractor with the upright blade? This blade can be considered as their plots, plans, and schemes that they devise behind your back to try and push or clear you out the way. Lastly, there could be people around you who view you as their obstacle, opposition, or opponent. When they see you trying to do something positive that feels like a threat to them, getting rid or disposing of you becomes their number one agenda. People like this will stick close to you in order to gain power over you by finding out your weaknesses. They seem to forget that the Bible says in 2 Corinthians 12:10, "Therefore I take pleasure in infirmities, in reproaches, in needs, in persecutions, in distresses for Christ's sake. For when I am weak, then I am strong." Our Father will give us the kind of strength that no one can bulldoze their way through. These three things will help you recognize the bulldozing backstabbers in your life. Seek them and remove them from your life immediately. Keep in mind that the Lord said, "no weapons formed against you shall prosper, and every tongue which rises against you in judgment You shall condemn. This is the heritage of the servants of the Lord, and their righteousness is from Me," Isaiah 54:17.

The Builders

Now let's discuss the builders in your life. I looked up two different definitions of builders to share with you. The first definition is exactly what it sounds like, which is someone who builds. The second definition is said to be a substance, such as an abrasive or filler, added to soaps or other cleaning agents to increase their effectiveness. I don't know about you ladies but I love anything that's going to help increase my effectiveness. So think about those in your circle whom you have granted access to your life. What person or people can you count on to be an abrasive or filler that adds to you increasing your effectiveness? The builders in your life are always trying to help you come up with new and improved strategies for that business you've always wanted to launch. They help build up your spirit after years of abuse or neglect. When that marriage and your children take a turn for the worse, they stand in prayer and agreement with you for things to get better. Philippians 2:4 reads, "Let each of you look out not only for his own interests, but also for the interests of others." This is what a builder in your life does for you. They look out for your interests along with their own. It's true when they say misery loves company. But a true builder in your life despises misery. They come around to help pull you out of misery instead of pushing you deeper into it.

Reflecting Moment: Think about these two totally different types of people. I want you to ask yourselves these next set of questions and give yourselves a true answer to each one. Who are the bulldozers in your life, and who are the builders? Why have you granted rooftop access to the bulldozers in your life? Most importantly, how long will you grant them access? When it comes to the builders in your life, what can you do to show them your appreciation if you haven't done so lately? Maybe you can call them up and express your gratitude. You could even take them out to lunch or dinner just to say thank you. We have so much to say about those who treat us unkindly. Why not switch things up and start showering the builders with kind words and gestures to show them just how much they are appreciated.

Rooftop Access: Access Denied

So, with all that being said, let's go back to the question I asked earlier. Do they have rooftop access? Nine times out of ten if they are projecting negativity and hatefulness towards you and others, they don't have rooftop access. In other words, their access has been denied by our Lord and Savior Jesus Christ because of their willingness to submit more to their hateful ways than to the ways of Christ. When people are coming at you in negative or hateful ways with their words and actions, it has nothing to do with you and everything to do with them. They are lacking in their walk with Christ. There's either something they're holding on to or something in their spirit that they are allowing to control them. Instead of recognizing it and giving it to God, they project their issues onto others. When we have a true relationship with our Lord and Savior Jesus Christ, His light shines in and upon us in such a way that people notice it. This can be seen by your positive attitude, the smile that you keep on your face, or even the encouraging words that you give to those who you come in contact with. Bulldozers tend to view this as weakness, but this couldn't be further from the truth. We are actually stronger than them because of our Lord and Savior who lives in us. 1 John 4:4 tells us that, "He who is in me is greater than he who is in the world."

Reflecting Moment: Sisters I would like to leave you with one last question for you to reflect on. If our Lord and Savior Jesus Christ has denied these bulldozers access to Him, why do you willingly grant them access to you? If their ways are unacceptable to Him then they should also be unacceptable to us. Access is granted to those who seek Him wholeheartedly. Psalms 119:2, Blessed are those who keep His testimonies, who seek Him with the whole heart! Deuteronomy 4:29, But from there you will seek the Lord your God, and you will find Him if you seek Him with all your heart and with all your soul. Matthew 7:8, For everyone who asks receives, and he who seeks finds, and to him who knocks it will be opened. Remember sisters that though we encounter bulldozers throughout our lives, our Father expects us to still treat them accordingly. Matthew 5:44 says, "But I say to you, love your enemies, bless those who curse you, do good to those who hate you, and pray for those who spitefully use you and persecute you." And for the builders in your life I leave you with this scripture from Job 42:10, And the Lord restored Job's losses when he prayed for his friends. Indeed, the Lord gave Job twice as much as he had before.

Bio/Conclusion

There are bulldozers who commit small offenses and some who commit bigger offenses. I've dealt with both. I was impacted in so many ways that sent me down a horrible path. After years of being stagnant and feeling unfulfilled I knew things had to change. I went back to school and got my G.E.D. to get started in the right direction. One day while lying in bed I prayed to my Heavenly Father and asked Him to show me how to be the mother that I was supposed to be. I no longer wanted my lack of knowledge in that area to hinder me in my role as a mother to my children. They deserved to have a much better version of me. The version that God intended me to be. My boyfriend at the time, who was and still is the best man I've ever dated, proposed to me and we got married. We moved in together and I went back to school to get my certified nursing assistant license. Taking care of people and loving others is something that I've always loved to do. Last year in May I went back to school again to perform sleep studies on those who suffer from sleep apnea and graduated March 29, 2019. I started writing in my first book as a co-author in March 2019 and it was published in August 2019. The very next month, in September, I started writing this book that I am also a co-author in. Two books in one year is truly a blessing. Though my Father in Heaven has blessed me with many accomplishments, I know I have not arrived. There are so many other avenues that He's going to take me down, grow me in and use me. So I continue to be humble, ask Him to teach me how to continue to grow as His servant, a wife, mother, writer, and business woman. Sisters let's keep pressing forward without looking back. Even though the sky's the limit, there is no limit to what God can do with us and through us. Find out who you are in Christ. Believe it and walk in it. Ask God these three questions. Why did you create me? What should I be doing? Who should I be doing it with? Make sure you ask with an expectation. In other words, expecting Him to answer you. Always remember ladies let your dreams be big but go after even bigger ones. Keep your faith high but still reach even higher. May God do exceedingly and abundantly above and beyond all that you can ask, see, or imagine. He's doing it for me, and I know He'll do it for you. God bless you all, my sisters Sarah. Those of you who would like to reach out to me can find me on Facebook as Sherica Thompson.

The Truth That Really Hurts

Siemone Anthony

Siemone Anthony is an aspiring Author. This will be the second book she has written. The first being Women to Women. As co Authored she has chosen to share her Inspirational journey and adventures by sharing the step to Greatness at face value. She has set the tone for her role in "Sister 's of Sarah as it applied to her journey

Her accomplishments include being an Entrepreneur, Poetry writing and Inspirational speaking. Siemone was a young single mother who not only worked hard to achieve goals that seemed to be unachievable. She has maintained a leadership role in just about every career she's had throughout the years.

Throughout this series you will find her at best as she gives us a little piece of herself with each section. You will have an opportunity to explore some of the strengths, the self motivation and Peace that has helped her through her life as she shares . The impact that life has on a person and the Integrity that allows her to indulge in what she has accomplished. This savvy, inspirational place is where you can plan on finding yourself needed more.

The Truth that Really Hurts

Genesis 17:16

I will bless her and will surely give you a son by her. I will bless her so that she will be the mother of nations; kings of peoples will come from her."

The strength Sarah needed to endure the consequences that were waiting on her must have been devastating, beyond the presence of the human sight. I think her level of Integrity to have strong morals and principles, no matter what the circumstances would truly be beyond reach this day in time. How the Sarah in my life pushed me to Finish the course. Despising the situation after making unwise decisions; headed in the wrong direction and realizing you have to turn around. Thinking it through. Once you have reached the degree of waiting that has weighed on your life it teaches you to make better decisions for your life and your family's life. Enough is enough I used to think I had to endure another person's shortcomings, problems and issues. Guess what! 'You don't.'' Don't allow people or things to interfere in the plans you have for your own life. If you decide to change the course make sure you can endure the circumstances that you will have to face. Taking responsibility for the decisions you make is a part of the steps. You can fill it up with your own trash. As you start to get rid of the things that are no longer of use to you: for example.

By choice I decided to take better control of my heart by stopping old habits and picking up a new way of doing things, like exercising, meditating and removing things and people that interfered with my growth out of my life.

New

Unfortunately, the confirmation is you. We are our own confirmation of who we think and know to be,

One day I was talking to a friend of mine. And he shared with me something about myself. It's not that it was a bad thing. It was an expression of what he has not only experienced with me, but has also watched over the years and saw the consistency of my behavior.

The point is, he was right on the spot. The characteristics that I have consistently shown have made it obvious in the sight of those who know me. I cannot hide who I really am. Not saying that I was! Enough is Enough.

I applaud the men and women Hungry for life, living it to the very fullest and persevering through hardship, high ship and controversy.

It appears that so many of us are lost in the opinion of others. Simply meaning that instead of taking what you have learned and knowing this for yourself: you allow others the privilege to dictate your move. Society tells everything we need to know. How much time do we spend finding out for ourselves?

Making a permanent decision, of a temporary circumstance

How do you know you are ready to elevate your life to the next level if you have not done absolutely NOTHING to prepare? God allows small tests in a Big blessing to happen in our life.

"It's not the situation that controls you; it's you that controls the situation.

One day I decided I needed to take the time to write down all the things that have negatively Impacted my life. When I was done, I was amazed by the things that I had written down. Not because of what had happened! The fact is, I am here today, stronger than ever, willing to take on life's adventures and to know that I have so much still to do. So I say , get yourself together allow yourself to obtain a visual of what you really want to happen in your life today. Snap out of " stuck in time" mode. Stop quitting before you even get started.

At times we all can attest to having the emotional experience of quitting something.

The planning, the preparation, the time, the effort, the energy, the compassion, the fight, and the steps in which you had to go through to get to where you are today.

Never look back and if you have to reflect don't linger very long. Stopping is not always a bad thing to do, reprioritizing your time to better utilize it is a genius idea. When things slow down around you and it feels like life is escaping you; reflect in the now and think about how far you have come? Because you are the one in control, you can see the situation a lot more clearly and that repeat that you thought you were on becomes a distant memory. Then give yourself a big treat for accomplishing the task of controlling your actions and knowing that being you is better than you could ever imagine.

Timing is everything

Mike Williams said in the book "Quality People"

If you do what is easy, your life will be hard.

If you do what is hard it will make your life Easy

Humility

Humility is a modest or low view of one's own importance.

I will ask the question, think about the words that describe Humility,

Shy, Low, unworthiness at some point we have all experienced spiral of unjustifiable emotion

When I was younger I allowed myself to fall onto a point of lowliness. My fear was that I would lash out from the mental and emotional

Aldos, Greek mythology, was the diamond (goddess) of shyness, shame, and humility. She was the quality that restrained Human beings from wrong

As a young mother I faced challenges beyond my own belief, but who could be a better critic about my actions other than ME.

Why do we put so much effort into pulling ourselves down? if you redirected the energy. imagine where YOU will be. Don't have self-pity, don't be ashamed of YOU and never accept less than what you know you deserve, at any time. I know it seems easier said than done, but nothing worth having is easy to obtain. If it were "then we wouldn't appreciate what we have or where we are in life. Once I accepted where I was in my life. I started making better decisions based on who I was. I started changing my mind set.I've always considered myself as a great listener but when you are experiencing your own personal moments in life The pull from those around you gets a bit aggressive. Life will try to knock you down from time to time and it will succeed, but you don't have to stay down. Sometimes we get frustrated with the people and the things around us, and we want to blame others for our own shortcomings. Own up to you, pay attention to the details of what you are experiencing in your life. If you are heading in the wrong direction there will be a small indication that you are headed for a possible repeat!! I'm here to tell you that you are experiencing some humility. Repeating bad behaviors is a magnet for repetition.

In Aww! I stand, honored and almost overwhelmed,

By the sound of Natures voice requesting my presence within.

The woman in me calls through the land to demand the presence of the heart of her man,

I yield to thee in peace Love and Respect.

Don't live in denial or fear! Always represent who you are. The person you see in the mirror is you and you are in total control. Yield to your own performance.

Recognizing your Gift and stepping into it. Armored up and prepared to exceed your own expectations.

Close Call

The mind experience

Is there something that you love doing, that you really can't share with anyone else? Whatever the pleasure, that you choose not to share?

Think about it, we spend most of our time mentally planning on how we can succeed in doing something that has not happened. It's called planning. I used to say I don't like making plans for the future, Because I never wanted to fail. I saw so many people fail and not succeed in their goals that they planned out so thoroughly

Why do we put so much effort into where we think we are going and very little into the moments of where we are going? If you never try then how will you ever know.

How many *close calls* have you had? I've had countless.

When you think you've seen that situation before; but not sure as something may have changed or maybe you just didn't see it coming. "Whatever your poison" it was just a *close call.*

Romans 12:2

Do not conform to the pattern of this world;

Be transformed by the renewing of the mind;

Then you will be able to test and prove what God's will is.

Hebrews 12:11

A changed mind

You can change all kinds of things in your life: for example where you live, the people you hang around with, your career, your hair color, etc... But if you do not *change your mindset,* you will continue having the same experience.

When you decide to change your mind, you will start having a different experience, a better experience.

At some point in our lives we have doubted our ability to follow through on life. The commitment you made to yourself. Did you follow through? Or did you just stop? Don't decrease your desire to win. You are not alone. Some see giving up as a choice and then later on in life get an "Ahh HAH moment" from it. Can you think of a time when you may have been in a relationship with someone and at that time in your life your mind was set on whether or not the situation was worth the fight? Your mind for tolerance should no longer exist in the area of REPEAT.

'Love is when you are kind, giving and understanding, Love is helpful'

The signs of a *changed mind* are when you start to realize that your life is changing and the people around you are different and trying something new is the ultimate solution

Finding Greatness

Greatness in Me

I know that my patients have awarded me the gift of hope. I was rewarded in Humility and in great affliction, Knowing my place in the Universe. I hold my head up in Grace and indulge in Adoration.

Try being in love with yourself. " If you do not believe you are GREAT; then who will"?

Psalm 13:12

Hope deferred maketh the heart sick — The delay of that which a man eagerly desires and expects is such an affliction, that it differs little from a lingering disease; but when the desire cometh — When the good desired and expected is obtained. It is a tree of life —

That is, most sweet, satisfactory, and reviving to the soul.

I suppose a lot of people use hope as an opportunity or even as an excuse to ignore the woes of life's adversities. What is your deferment? What are you hoping for?

Are you persevering through your crisis and healing through humility?

It's okay to Humble yourself, actually it's a Blessing to realize that being Humble doesn't mean you have failed or have given up on your Goals in life. The key is to treat everyone with love, believe in your ability. To give yourself some undivided attention, I'm sure it will be well deserved.

Maybe your Humbling will come once you begin to realize that God uses everyone that you help you.

The humility that is experienced tends to follow you.

Once I realized that my circumstances are sometimes a sign that Repeat is on its way, I began to take

a U-turn in the opposite direction. My goodness, If you are not paying attention to what is in front of you. You may pass up a very valuable listen that later on impacted your ability to live a part of Gods expectation for your life. If you notice I said IMPACTED! I say that with great respect for those who know exactly where I am coming from and deep heartfelt compassion for those who hardly ever embrace the reality of hope. You see the opportunity is always there we are just not always in a position to receive it.

Jeremiah 1:5

Before I formed you in the womb, I knew you, before you were born, I set you apart; I appointed you as a prophet to the Nation'

Missed Opportunity

The blessing is in humility. I remember a time I felt as though I was very miss understood. I tried numerous times over many years mixed with a lot of time and energy to explain myself; until one day it came to me. that no matter who I said I was; some people are just not on the same level and some things are just not supposed to happen.

Are you paying attention to what you need in your life. I never imagined I would be in a situation where I actually felt vulnerable enough to allow myself to end up recognizing some very familiar places with unhealthy behaviors that caused a lot of hardship for me. In all that we desire to change we have waiting in front of us, Greatness! Sometimes we have to wait out the circumstances.

No matter how many times an act is repeated to mimic someone else it will never be the same, each time is always different. When I found myself in a familiar place I realized, there must have been something that I just didn't get, certainly I missed something. I was convinced that it was necessary for me to see the repetitive behavior in my life that was unhealthy for my growth, from the food s that I ate to the places I traveled.

If you notice you are repeating the same things over and over then do something about it. Tell yourself it's not going to happen. Believe in you, know that you are the prize. Capture the moment and then start making some Great memories for the rest of your life. If your life was a snapshot of a photo that captured the eyes of people from all over the world; would you consider that as Greatness? One shall not hope for change with the assumption that change doesn't come without growing pains, they are inevitable. As we go through life and time proceeds you, change begins to happen, take what you have learned and keep moving forward in life. Use all resources available to you and for you. Don't try making sense out of someone else's NON -sense- make better choices for your life. Go for Greatness.

Leave the things and the people that have now become a stunt in your growth and tell it 'Goodbye'. Run in the opposite direction and leave the past behind. What works for me, doesn't always work for everyone, but I am a witness to process, the steps and the rewards. Use your circumstances as an opportunity.

Take a moment, reflect on the wonderful people you have met and all the perfect moments that ended up giving another person just what they needed. The effortless task of just being the wonderful person that you are. Self-motivation is the Greatest motivation you possess, who knows you better than you?

The magnitudes of awareness should elevate you to continue to strive for Greater things.

When you focus on Solutions you attract Opportunity'

Reality Check

Most of you may be very familiar with the saying "Don' t put certain things in the atmosphere because once out there someone else will grab it". My all-time favorite " You reap what you sow'. Listen, I live by these two statements, not just because I've heard this most of my use, I've lived it for my life. I will continue to do that today. The manner in which it Impacts my life is the big difference.

Let me just say, I have arrived! I am so Thankful that God has blessed me in a place of consciousness. Surround yourself with people who really love themselves, because those are the people that will also love you ". Birds of a feather ' flock together, Right?

What is your drive? I know you expected a different answer, but the truth in this matter is that the more you love YOU! The more you love others and the more you share that love. No regrets; remember? It seems like there's a lot of questions that we sometimes need to ask ourselves; you know the drill, just a short recap or maybe a quick overview would suffice. I have come to know one thing for sure about my own life.; I can't assume that another person will think of me ,the same way I think of myself. That would clearly be a huge mistake. At times we should question our decisions. Challenge yourself to an extent of correcting our own mistake, appreciating your own failures and knowing that because you persevered you can see the outcome and because you are in control of making your own decisions, whether good or bad, respect starts at the person you look at everyday of your life. Stop making decisions without thinking them through.' What is your Sarah? People put a lot of time and effort into making someone else' s life miserable without a doubt; by making poor choices and not being patient enough to work through the problem and then very little time giving positive energy and trying to help others I remember a time when I felt so defeated. It was like I was all alone in the world. I learned very early in life that everyone's rock bottom is very different. My rock-bottom was when I was a victim of domestic violence several times. Each time I entered a relationship, that allowed myself the gift of loving as unconditionally as I possibly could. I was not patient enough to allow God to take me through the steps. Everyone has a solution to someone else's problem.

My life transformed by controlling my thoughts and actions. I just gave into the time it took and I would sit and think of ways to fix the problem. Physical abusive, verbal abuse and of course my all-time favorite and kept forgiving, before I realized that I could just walk away. Not because I thought lowly of myself but because my heart cried out for God to have Mercy on me and mostly him. My ability to avoid the situation was much easier to attain. I was at my lowest point or at least, I thought I was.

When I realized that my gift was so very valuable that if I did not protect myself it would be on a long repetitive path. Why are we so bothered by the unknown? For me, I have no fear of the unknown or what "might" happen but I must admit I am somewhat at aww!! At the making decision on if you choose to deal with the consequences of the path they were chosen, can somewhat be a mystery."No regrets" .Right?.

Sometimes we get carried away with what might have been; then we forget that we no longer live in that time. The past exists within as well as our future. Make your choices meaningful. Stop using what you are trying to leave behind as an excuse to bring with you as you step into your future. If past behavior shows up, you show it out. Never let anything keep you from being the Awesome, Extraordinary being that you are. Sounds clichéé' well it should, don't kid ourselves. Things happen in life that are out of our control, it is up to you to do what you can about your situation.

To be tried, in which your actions may affect others or people that are close to you, but mean nothing to you. Hebrews 12:4 The supply of substances that we obtain from God is beyond one's imagination

Finish the Course

For unto whomsoever much is given of him shall be much required'

Luke 12:47

I am an essential part of the universe

I am indispensable. No one can ever take my place.

I am light,

I am peace,

I am Love

I am Joy,

I am hope,

I am compassion

I am health

I am knowledge

I am Me,

I am forgiveness

I am ME

The words you speak into your life; Come to life!

'when you focus on opportunity you attract opportunities

You have a right to question your own mind. Why wouldn't you? For me it opens an opportunity to learn more about myself. In the world today, there is nothing that you can't find out. The technology is at an all-time high. We are able to activate the appliances in our home from our workplaces and monitor your alarm system from thousands of miles away. When you think you can't go any further; wherever you are in life , stop for a minute and take the time to assess the situation, you will have a clear view, when you see how you can assist ; use that energy, that time that very moment to relate to your thoughts: are in control . Know that you are the prize. Every time you choose to move "past the PAST ". Take ownership to correct yourself. I don't proclaim to know everything, but I Definitely know a lot about me. When I am going through day by day, Indulging in the hustle and bustle of everyday life , I take time to explore other options in my life. As I get older I see that the right to change my mind Is also the right that I have given myself to take the things I can from my past and continue to move forward until I reach the finish line. Using my time wisely seems to be very rewarding for me. I used to think the busier that I am, the better off was to stay busy all the time and then I realized it.

Get up every day and know that the effort it took for you to RISE up is the perfect start of your day. What does it take for you to RISE up?

Sometimes you have to -dig in and just be thankful for all that God has done for you for your life and your children's life, thankful for the battles he has continued to fight for you.

God I was doing the right thing ... Difficult situations to prove to you he is GOD. He could have saved Daniel from the lion's Den. Sometimes God will allow things to happen in your life for others to see because it's not about you it's about the people around you

Deuteronomy 1;11

May the Lord God of your fathers make you a thousand times more than you are. How many times have you heard someone say " If you want things to be different; you have to change what you are doing, same action, same results. I stopped being on the receiving side of that comment and started sharing those very words with others.

The circumstances are what they are, get over it. It is always your choice to move forward or stay where you are in life. I have told myself since I was a young woman: there are 3 things I will share in life.

1. Make choices that you will not Regret. I know that seems impossible., However, you only achieve what you choose to believe. Choose to CARE not because someone told you too, or you heard or read a story about. Choose to CARE because it gives your life to share what you have with others who have a need for what you possess

Choose to believe in yourself, have confidence in being just who you think you are? believe that what can happen has already happened before and can happen again.

It almost seems like an unreachable goal to achieve. But because it is you that sets the tone, explore the things that you have never experienced before.

The saying goes. "If you can talk the talk, you can walk the walk

In my previous writings I talked about being Consistent; the gift of accuracy and fairness. Acting in the same manner having the same Quality.

Once you have established behaviors in your life you can began to see what you are holding on to and the consistencies you have made your self-belief is a part of that fairness and accuracy, by acting in the same manner then you have identified some things that you have grown to think is a part of a normal action for your life.

Growth comes with a price and if you're willing to grow then you are up for the challenge? A few years ago I was speaking at a women's conference, so it happened to be an opportunity to ask the very same question. ARE you up for the CHALLENGE? Some may think the question is a bit rhetorical, as one should. It really is, but it's also inevitable.

Who said you have to do the same thing all the time. This is the challenge that a lot of people have; I can attest to that. Challenge yourself to do better in not just loving yourself but getting to know you. At the end of the day when you have done all that you can do. Then what is next? Can you finish the course? Be confident in your ability to succeed.

The steps are everything and they are an essential part of our own growth. Have you ever stopped to think how important we all are to one another?

Take some time and think about how really important you are to the universe.

At what point do you stop to think about how important we are to one another and how the choices we make for ourselves, will utterly impact our loved ones lives.

I remember times when I was making decisions solely based on where I was at that time in my life with no regards to anyone else. However, at the end of the day, I thought about my future and my children's future often. When you are young, single and trying to raise children as a single parent it made me that I was not fully living up to the best of my ability. I had failed to meet my own expectations.

I had to start loving myself for who I truly was to discover my PURPOSE in life. I had to embrace my PURPOSE, so I could begin to evolve above

Do you know the difference between a Goal and Hope? My mom asked me that one day and I was someone perplexed about the question and then it came to me.

I can remember a time when I thought I had finally gotten to a place in my life where I thought that I had it all figured out, until I realized I didn't. I just finished the course and Began a*nother'*.

Sisters of Sarah

Stolen Time

Talesiya Calton

Many people think young adults should not have to worry about anything in life.

It is true that we go through things just like the rest of the adults. There were times in my life that people would judge me because I appeared to be an inexperienced teenager. This caused them to take me for granted. Before I share my story, I want to encourage you as the reader with this. "The Only way you can recognize you are treating someone this way is by evaluating your own behavior and mindset." If done correctly you can help young adults see life circumstances clearly.

"Don't let anyone despise your youth, but set an example for the believers in speech, in conduct, in love, in faith, and in purity." Timothy 4:12

Transitioning into my young adulthood I was fractured mentally and emotionally. Over the previous years I've been dealing with an individual who had total control over me, not physically but emotionally and mentally. However, God has given me many chances to get away from this individual but then again I was not ready to let go. I was at a point in my life that I believed this individual loved me. "How would I know about love, besides I'm only eighteen."

Mentally, I thought I knew what real love was all about. I would spend most of my day talking to this individual missing valued time with my family, because I thought I knew it all. I was too busy giving all my time to this toxic relationship. In turn, I would be mean to my siblings for no reason. I would neglect the precious moments I could have made with friends and because I was so occupied, I had no genuine relationships.

Colossians 3:20

"Children, obey your parents in all things: for this is well pleasing unto the Lord."

Honesty, while getting lost in this individual relationship it caused me to lose focus and it eventually blocked my blessings in life. When you look at the above scripture you will see how important it is to listen to your parents. For instance, it stopped me from getting a car and getting my drivers license. I had to do things on my own such as buying my own clothes, shoes and pay my own phone bill. Although I was losing sight, I was gaining my way in real adult life. No matter how hard it was to realize my faults the up side to this is that this experience helped me become an independent young adult.

As a teen going into adulthood, I was expecting to be spoiled just a little longer before actually leaving home.

Moving forward, I was getting deeper into this relationship and my focus was to be with this individual for the rest of my life but my main focus should have been being closer to God and my family.

During this time, I was having trouble figuring out my major in college, I quit sports and worked less because all I wanted was time with this individual. The sad thing is that I was pursuing him and he was not pursuing me.

Matthew 6:20

"But lay up for yourselves treasures in heaven, where neither moth nor rust doth corrupt, and where thieves do not break through nor steal." This scripture became one of my favorites during the time of attending camps and bible studies I would lean on Matthews words.

Recently, I had no choice but to let go. God had blessed My family and I to move to the state of Montana. Which definitely shook some things up. Although, there are several ways to communicate I was so thankful that the lord made another way to escape this situation. At times I would just sit alone in a dark room, because I could not see the light of God. Reflecting now, all I had to do was open the door of my heart and hear God. Instead, I was only hearing my own voice. Leaving Texas was the primary thing that helped me get myself back in the word of god and in my family life.

Psalms 139:24

"And see if there is any wicked way in me, and lead me in the way everlasting."

It wasn't easy for this transition, now I have actually become closer to God.

God has helped me when I couldn't help myself. I thought I could help myself and make myself better but it just would not work out. God showed how life or even a person can lead you to destruction. I had so many opportunities from God and this time I took it.

My parents would tell me things that would convict my heart but I would totally ignore it and we should never ignore anything from God especially when He is using our parents.

God will send people into your life to save your life. My great grandmother used to tell my father "listen this might save your life." That's the truth listen, to whoever is guiding you in the right direction. God said train up a child the way they should go.

Some days it is hard to know that my life could have been a breeze but instead I took a disobedient path. As a result, I feel I have to catch up. I am willing to make it better with God, my family and myself.

So I'm encouraging you to look around and evaluate the people around you. Are they positive or negative individuals? Are they a follower of Christ or a follower of the world? It is okay if you lose a friend or a relationship with a relative. Because you are doing the will of God. Know that this is the right thing to do and the best thing you could ever do with your life. Many people believe you cannot have fun with your friends and family in Christ but that is not true. I'm a Christian and I still have fun in the most respectful way.

Listen, we are all humans and we make mistakes and that's okay.

Hebrews 11:16 " But as it is, they desire a better country, that is, a heavenly one. Therefore, God is not ashamed to be called their God, for he has prepared for them a city."

Just remember every day is not promised to us so we have to do what is best for us and our family. Our goal is to get into heaven and spend our eternal life with Christ, help others around us and teach them about Christ. It is important to have a relationship with God. He is our creator, He has made us in his own image, and for his purpose.

It is up to us to know what that purpose is. Let's not spend our time wasting on unvalued and toxic people.

Romans 6:23 For the wages of sin is death, but the free gift of God is eternal life in Christ Jesus our Lord.

The question is how do we get into heaven? Where do we start? Well first you have to hear the gospel, if you believe then move forward with being baptized and then you will receive the gift from God (Holy Spirit), Acts 2:38.

This does not mean you cannot or will not make mistakes. It means that as long as you turn from sin and stop purposely making mistakes God will forgive you. Enjoy every moment of your life.

It is never too late to say yes to Christ!

Sisters of Sarah

Battered, Bruised and Broken

Luwanna Riles

Battered, Bruised & Broken: Victim to Victor!

Battered, bruised and broken I tried to hold on to what I thought was the love of my life, while slowly losing life. Trying to hold back the tears, and fight through my fears, that stole irreversible years. Battered, bruised and broken, losing in an unnecessary fight not worth anyone's life...not even MINE!

I had no idea that I was battered, bruised or even broken, until the day I laid on my living room floor weak, in pain, barely able to lift my head up and body almost lifeless. At that moment I had no clue as to what would happen next, yet I heard the words of my abuser, "Look what you made me do to you". Badly beaten, I had one last prayer, one last wish...God please let me survive. Let me live!

The physical abuse was not something that happened on a regular basis or often enough to considerably be a problem, at least that's how I viewed the situation at the time. I dealt with it when it happened, by not dealing with it and not admitting that the man I loved and whom I was married to, had a problem and needed help. I also needed help. There are many complex reasons for not seeking help from an abusive relationship (domestic violence) and in the last few sentences, I've just told you one of the most common...acceptance of the situation and not admitting there is a problem. Blinded by what I knew to be love, I feel extremely vulnerable to not just sporadic domestic violence, but also to every devoted apology that followed. The abuse was so far spread out and apart. I thought I knew how to handle it. I was convinced that if I prayed harder, longer, and invariably, that things would get better. I insisted on making HIM better, more lovable and everything I could have wanted and hoped for in a mate. Sadly to say, that my prayers did not seem effective. My inner scars outnumbered my prayers. Lying to myself, I kept on believing that there would be a life-changing moment when my marriage would take a turn for the better and be blissful again. So satisfying a need to stay in an unhealthy marriage because of fear, embarrassment and for the children, I stayed "a little while longer". A little while longer is the amount of time I knew it was going to take to make things better. But a little while longer was taking longer and longer.

There was one New Year's Day, I had asked him to leave the house and to leave me alone. He stated that it was his house and he wasn't going anywhere. So, I told him I was leaving. He replied to me the words, "What? You think you're going to leave me?" That very moment he jumped up off the couch and ran across the house to the room. I knew he was going for his gun. So, I ran for the front door. The bar door was locked. As he came around the corner with a gun pointed in my face, there was nothing I could think to do or say at that moment. My daughters ran out of their rooms from playing and asked if I was okay. He then hides the gun in the back of his pants. The only thing I could think of at that moment is God please don't let him shoot and kill me in front of the girls. I somehow felt and really knew in my heart that he wouldn't harm them or harm me in front of them. Once I said, "mommy's okay", the oldest ran back to play in her room. And my heart dropped. The youngest one however, wrapped her arms around my leg. I saw an evilness in his eyes that frightened me terribly. I told my baby I was okay and told her to go into the room with her sister. He drew the gun on me again. Raising his voice, he asked me to repeat what I said. He wanted me to repeat that I was leaving him.

I turned towards him, face-to-face. I told him these words. "I think I've been the best friend, companion and wife to you and the best mother that I know how to those children. I know I've hurt some people, but I've helped a whole lot more. I know I've done some bad things in my life, but I've done more good. I know that if you kill me right now, I'll be absent from this body but instantly present with the Lord. But as for you, you're going to have to answer to God for this!" I remember turning my back on him, walking away and stepping down in the family room (den). All within a few seconds, I stood still and looked around the corner into the laundry room towards the back door, in which I planned on trying to get out. Yet, I heard nothing. There was deafening silence. Having not heard the gun go off and me not getting shot, afraid to turn around, I did. What I saw was a man holding a gun in his hand and mouth open, as in disbelief. I think he was in shock that I [finally] stood up to him. I marked the day as "The Day I Stood Up to The Devil".

You may be going through something like this or know someone who is, and I want you to know that YOU or THAT person can survive and get out! Fear can be defeated! I had finally defeated fear! And I'll tell anyone, so can they. You've got to know that Faith and Fear cannot exist together. Faith is described in Hebrews 11:1 as being "certain of what we do not see." It is an absolute belief that God is constantly working behind the scenes and in our favor, in every area of our lives, even when there is no tangible evidence to support that fact. When I lived in fear all those years, I allowed unbelief to gain the upper hand in my thoughts. Fear took hold of my emotions. Understanding that my deliverance from fear and worry was solely based on faith, which is the opposite of unbelief. Faith is not something that we can produce in ourselves. Faith is a gift (Ephesians 2:8-9), and faithfulness is described as a fruit (or characteristic) that is produced in our lives by the Holy Spirit (Galatians 5:22-23).

As a believer, our faith is a confident assurance in a God who loves us, who knows our thoughts, and who cares about our deepest needs. Although I lived through this, I never lost faith or my belief in God, I lost faith in myself (low self-esteem). My faith began to grow the more I desired to get out of the situation and desired God's will for my life. My faith began to grow the more I desired God's love and happiness. My faith began to grow every time I looked into the eyes of my two young daughters. God wasn't going to help me until I helped myself. A growing faith is what we all should desire to have and what God desires to produce in us. But how, in day-to-day life, can we develop a faith that conquers our fears? The answer is simply found in Romans 10:17, which says, "Faith comes by hearing, and hearing by the Word of God." God is kind and understanding toward our weaknesses. With God, you can triumph over any situation. Victory belongs to YOU! You could have experienced being battered, bruised or broken, just know that in the end you went from VICTIM to VICTOR!

Elder Luwanna S. Riles

I was born in Camden, New Jersey. She spent most of her childhood in beautiful San Diego, California and later moved to Miami, Florida. She now resides in Miami Gardens, Florida. Her formal education was given through the MDCPS system, where she is a graduate and alumni of Miami Northwestern Senior High School. Elder LuWanna Riles is currently in school pursuing her goals in Christian Education, aspiring to become a Christian Clinical Psychologist.

Elder LuWanna Riles, is a member of **The Point 317** (formerly known as Truth Worship Center), under the leadership of Bishops James & Overseer Dr. Jacqueline Wright. Elder Riles serves in many capacities: Bishop James Wright's City Church Fellowship administrator, President of the Pastor Aide Board, Director of Christian Education, Chaplain of The Point 317 Bible Institute, Sunday School Superintendent, Sunday School Adult class teacher, Assistant to Children's Ministry Pastor and member of The Point 317 Singles Ministry.

Having crossed many bridges and walked through red seas, Elder Riles daringly and boldly continues to carry her cross into the enemy's camp, proclaiming the Gospel of Jesus Christ. Her favorite scripture, Luke 12:48, ***"For unto whomsoever much is given, of him shall be much required"***.

Sisters of Sarah

ABOUT THE AUTHOR

Nadia Watson-Anthony

Nadia Watson- Anthony was born on August 1, 1984 in Fort Worth, Texas. She is a faithful teacher of the Gospel, dedicated wife and mother of nine, marriage counselor and life coach. She is a Graduate of Sunset Bible Institution holding a degree in Biblical studies. Nadia puts her degree to work by traveling the world, speaking to groups of women who feel as though they have lost their power. Nadia is also a graduate of Amridge University with a Bachelor's of Science in Business Management. With this degree she became the Founder of H.E.R Inspiration, a service that searches for a woman and gives them an equal opportunity to be an inspiration to the world through their book writing. In 2019 Nadia collaborated eight-teen women who became Co-authors, giving them an opportunity to write in her Anthology "Woman to Woman."

Nadia is currently pursuing her Master's degree in Social Services looking to service her community in the masses. Nadia is the founder of Christian Maturity Mentorship Program, she's a sponsor for the American Foundation for Suicide Prevention, she supports a Mission (yearly ladies' day) in Togo West Africa, she is a Book writing Representative for Greatness University of London, UK. Nadia has written several books, *"H.E.R. Inspiration 31 day devotion," "Women to Women "transitioning into your best future," "Woman to Woman Sisters of Sarah," "The Book of Love"* and has co-author varies of books *(BEST SELLERS)*

"Jesus changed our lives" and *"Les Brown changed our lives"* In between traveling Nadia volunteers to for speaking engagements at nursing facilities and schools. Nadia is passionate about all creation, education, leadership, empowerment and her faith. Nadia believes that everyone should at least write one book in their lifetime. Nadia can be found on all social sites, Instagram:author_nadiaanthony,rep_greatnessuniversity and facebook, Anthony's bond.

"In order to be a great Individual, one must read and educate themselves on all areas of life."-Nadia Anthony

Prayer: Dear Lord, thank You for ensuring that I am followed by Your goodness and mercy for the rest of my life. You are the shepherd who guides me to the good parts of life; so, Lord, I thank You. I thank You that it is You who satisfies my soul and fills me with Your goodness, forever and ever. So, I bless You for the goodness that I am promised now and in the future. Lord I love You and thank You in advance, Amen.

Thank you for reading my Anthology! Please check out my social sites for what I'm working on, or contact me at: writeabookwithnadia@outlook.com

Sisters of Sarah